PUBLIC ACCESS

MICROCOMPUTERS

IN ACADEMIC LIBRARIES

The Mann Library Model

at Cornell University

Edited by
Howard Curtis

Contributors:

Katherine Chiang
Bill Coons
Howard Curtis
Samuel Demas
Joan Lippincott

James Madden
Mary Ochs
Jan Olsen
Linda Stewart

AMERICAN LIBRARY ASSOCIATION
Chicago and London 1987

Cover designed by Kay Hartmann

Composed by Katherine Chiang
        in Times using PageMaker
        and Word software on an Apple
        Macintosh with a LaserWriter.

Printed on 50-pound Warren's 1854,
        a pH-neutral stock, and bound
        in 10-point Carolina cover stock by
        McNaughton & Gunn, Inc.

Library of Congress Cataloging-in-Publication Data

Public access microcomputers in academic libraries.

    Includes index.
    1. Albert R. Mann Library. 2. Microcomputers--
Library applications--Case studies. 3. Libraries,
University and college--Automation--Case studies.
4. Information retrieval--Case studies. 5. Libraries
and readers--Case studies. 6. Library science--Data
processing--Case studies. 7. Library orientation--Case
studies. I. Curtis, Howard.
Z733.A33P83 1987 027.7747'71 86-22315
ISBN 0-8389-0464-5

This book is dedicated to the staff
of Mann Library, whose efforts have made the
programs of the Microcomputer Center a possibility.
It is also dedicated to the student employees of the
Microcomputer Center. Their enthusiasm and hard work
have done much to make these programs a success.

Contents

Preface

This book describes one university library's experiment with a public-access microcomputer center. It also presents a particular viewpoint on the role of microcomputers in the academic library, as tools of information access, retrieval, and control. Because of these two elements, there is a tension throughout between the particular and the general, between the practical application and the theoretical base.

Although we highlight what is of common interest to the library and academic community, the points we seek to make in the chapters that follow oblige us to describe the specific circumstances of our library-- Mann Library-- at Cornell University.

We have included details about our situation for several reasons. First, on one level this is an account of why one library concluded that it should build a microcomputer center, how it went about establishing the center, and how its computer facility relates to the collections and instructional programs of the library. For any library that plans to install a microcomputer facility and hopes to gain by what we have to say on the topic, it will be important to understand how our decision making derived from our environment at Cornell so that adjustments can be made for the particulars of another institution. Second, the nine people who have contributed chapters to this work represent almost half the professional staff of Mann Library. The background they bring to the book, though it may emanate from certain theories of information transfer and librarianship, is anything but abstract. All are writing about their working lives over the past two years. Finally, it was the feeling of our publisher that a description of the creation and management of a public-access microcomputer facility, based on the real experiences of a working library, would be more thought-provoking and useful than a manual of abstract prescriptions.

Precisely because libraries must answer the needs of their own constituencies and institutions, a microcomputer facility in another library, academic or otherwise, may well offer an entirely different spectrum of services than ours does. Still, many of the lessons we have learned in creating and administering a microcomputer center will be of broad interest in the library community. The central hypothesis of this book--that microcomputers present libraries with an innovative and affordable technology that enables library professionals to rethink and radically change the ways in which they provide access to the information in their "collections," convey that information to patrons, and teach patrons to control scholarly information for themselves--is generally applicable, and at all points our program derives from this idea.

Acknowledgments

Although every book is undoubtedly the work of many people, few involve quite the group effort that gave rise to this one. Nine members of the staff of Mann Library contributed directly to the writing of the chapters that appear here. These nine authors represent the Collection Development, Public Services, and Technical Services departments of the library, as well as the Information Technology Section--the unit that administers the Mann Library Microcomputer Center.

As this "diffuse" authorship indicates, one of our principal goals in establishing the Microcomputer Center at Mann Library was to broadly integrate public-access microcomputing into the programs of an academic library. Because this integration was our objective, and because we have made substantial progress toward its achievement, it would be fair to say that while the nine staff members who wrote this book are their visible representatives, the entire staff of the library helped bring the Microcomputer Center to its present form.

Several members of the library staff other than the chapter authors do deserve mention for specific contributions to this work. Christine Sherratt, our Instructional Librarian and the Public Services professional who has coordinated the end-user instructional program for the past 18 months, reviewed Chapters 9 and 10 and made many valuable suggestions. Chris also compiled figures on the scope of our workshops for the chapters on the instructional program. Mary Kelly, Administrative Manager of the library, has kindly reviewed the sections of the text that refer to university purchasing procedures and assisted with the fiscal and bureaucratic issues which a project like this book inevitably generates, and which appear insoluble until they are taken up by someone as familiar with the workings of the university as she. Kari Blinn, who started her career at Mann Library as a student assistant in the Microcomputer Center, until stolen away for "the book," contributed her considerable and consistent energies for the better part of an academic year to the typing, correction, and recorrection of the manuscript. After Kari's graduation, Amanda Buckley stepped in and carried the manuscript to completion, mastering the intracacies of desktop publishing in the process. Without their efforts we would not have emerged with a publishable product. Susan Ryan and Carolyn VanderWeide also contributed to the completion of the manuscript.

Katherine Chiang and Linda Stewart, two of the chapter authors, were responsible for the production of the index. Kathy supervised the production of the final camera-ready version of the manuscript.

In addition to those who have worked so hard at Mann Library to bring this book to press, thanks are due to numerous others who contributed to the project. The material on the administrative and computing environment at Cornell, which appears in the Introduction, derives from personal experience and also from a series of interviews conducted with university and college administrators, faculty members, and staff of Cornell Computer Services. Those who generously consented to contribute in this way were George Conneman, Mary Margaret Fischer, Ronald Furry, Gordon Galloway, Keith Kennedy, Kenneth King, William Trochim, and Agelia Velleman. John Rudan, Assistant Vice Provost for Computing, provided figures on microcomputer sales at Cornell. Tom Hughes of Decentralized Computer Services and Alan Personius of Network Communications reviewed drafts of the Introduction. Nancy Saltford, Associate Dean of the College of Human Ecology, made many valuable suggestions concerning the content of Chapter 1.

To Bettina MacAyeal, Associate Editor at the American Library Association, must go the credit for suggesting that Mann Library undertake this project in the first place. Suggestion is one thing, however, and execution another. At every stage in the preparation of this manuscript, Ms. MacAyeal has been at once the library's greatest fan and our most perceptive critic. There is not a chapter in this book that is not substantially better for her careful reading and acute editorial eye.

There remains one person whose overall contribution to the Mann Microcomputer Center and to this book should be introduced here because her "slight" presence in the chapters that follow is deceptive. Jan Olsen, Director of the library, has reviewed all the chapter drafts for the book and made perceptive suggestions for the modification of at least four. Even more important, the role she played in conceptualizing, creating, and developing the programs of the Microcomputer Center was critical, as it has been in almost every program the library has undertaken in the past four years. Without her enthusiasm, persuasiveness, and leadership, there not only would be no book-- there would be no Microcomputer Center at Mann Library.

Introduction

Mann Library, which commands the eastern end of the "Ag Quad"--one of Cornell's three large quadrangles of academic buildings--was built in the early 1950s using plans that were put together before the Depression. With its massive facade, cavernous reading rooms, and high ceilings, the library mixes handsome Art Deco touches with a certain Stalinesque grandeur.

Although smaller than the central research library (the John M. Olin Library), Mann Library is the largest of the 15 "branch" libraries at Cornell University. Mann is a considerable library in its own right. With holdings in excess of 550,000 volumes and an acquisitions rate of approximately 11,000 volumes per year, it is second in size only to the National Agricultural Library among agricultural libraries in the United States. The staffing level fluctuates between 50 and 60, with 23 full-time professionals. Together with all the Cornell libraries, Mann belongs to the Research Libraries Group and uses the RLIN system for cataloging, acquisitions, and interlibrary loan.

The library's mission is to support the programs of research, instruction, and cooperative extension within four academic units at Cornell--the College of Agriculture and Life Sciences, the College of Human Ecology, the Division of Biological Sciences, and the Division of Nutritional Sciences. The College of Agriculture and Life Sciences (CALS) and the College of Human Ecology (CHE) are two of Cornell's four "statutory" (state) colleges. As the statutory units, unlike the private (endowed) components of Cornell, have legal and contractual obligations to the state university system of New York and draw much of their funding from SUNY, Mann Library has official standing among the libraries of the SUNY research universities. Because Cornell was originally a land-grant institution, the library also takes its place among the land-grant colleges and universities of the United States.

Given the academic orientation of its clientele, Mann is primarily a science library with emphasis on such fields as agronomy, the life sciences, biotechnology, and nutrition. It also has important collection strengths in other diverse areas, including consumer economics and human development.

The library supports a research faculty that makes frequent use of its collections. In addition, Mann serves an undergraduate population of about 5,000 students. The library handles approximately 200,000 loans annually from its circulation desk and another 180,000 transactions through a busy reserve operation.

In 1982, with a change in administration, Mann Library began to stress automation and innovative public services programs among its major goals. The Microcomputer Center and the services it supports, which form the subject of this book, are one concrete product of the new direction.

An awareness of the administrative implications of the institutional framework in which Mann Library operates may be useful to the reader of the chapters that follow. Cornell is an unusually decentralized institution, divided as it is into state and private components, so that the individual colleges and professional schools of the university exercise great independence and initiative. Because its constituent colleges and divisions make the funding decisions that affect the library, Mann enjoys a scope for independent action that far exceeds what is typical for a university "branch" library. Although there is intense competition for financial resources within the colleges, their administrations will back ambitious capital projects if convinced of their value.

In addition to the broad administrative backdrop of Cornell and its colleges, the programs of the Microcomputer Center complement those of the other organizations and facilities that support academic computing at Cornell. The remainder of the Introduction will describe this computing environment, which has changed dramatically in the last several years. As suggested in the Preface, this information may assist the reader in comparing our circumstances with those found in another institution.

COMPUTING AT CORNELL

The organization that supports computing at Cornell (Cornell Computer Services), like those at many universities, has grown over the last decade to a scale that compares with the university libraries in complexity, number of staff, and budget. Again, like their equivalents at most institutions, the libraries and the computing center are separately administered, although, in part as a result of library automation planning, they now cooperate much more closely than they have in the past. There have begun to be heard suggestions that university administration should work to bring the two units even closer together.

In the last five years, three major trends have emerged in academic computing at Cornell which affect the Microcomputer Center at Mann Library. First, microcomputers have become extremely prevalent on a campus that five years ago did almost all its computing on the university mainframe computers. Second, the "circle of instruction" in computing has broadened dramatically. The third important trend is a decentralization of computing support throughout the university.

THE MOVEMENT TO MICROCOMPUTERS

The first public-access microcomputers appeared at Cornell in September 1980. During the academic year 1980-81, 23 TERAK microcomputers--equipped with disk drives larger than the system units of many current generation micros--were introduced in two campus computer facilities that previously had contained only terminals on the mainframe system. Faculty members employed these machines to teach programming technique, with the language PL/1, in an introductory course in computer science.

In January 1982, Decentralized Computer Services (DCS), a new unit of Cornell Computer Services responsible for microcomputer support and the investigation of emerging technologies, began to offer consulting support for a machine called the Apple II. Although demand quickly developed for consulting about microcomputers, the majority of the staff of Computer Services remained unconvinced that the microcomputer was the wave of the future.

DCS began to offer direct sale of microcomputers to the campus community in February 1982. By early 1983, Cornell had arranged "deep discounts" with three vendors of microcomputers--Apple, DEC, and IBM. By offering excellent prices on machines manufactured by these companies, Computer Services managed to concentrate departmental purchases of microcomputers on a fixed number of hardware configurations, rationalizing what would otherwise have become an impossible job of user support.

By late 1983, the full extent of the movement to microcomputing was becoming obvious. The capabilities of microcomputers were increasing almost monthly, prices were dropping, and the machines were appearing in large numbers across campus. When the Department of Computer Science decided to move three of its largest programming courses to the Apple Macintosh beginning fall semester 1984, Computer Services had to scramble to find space for 80 Macintoshes in public facilities.

The Macintosh also had the effect, psychologically and financially, of pushing students from all walks of academic life to microcomputing. Over the course of the two years that began in July 1984, Network Communications, which assumed the sales function for microcomputers from DCS, sold more than 3,800 Macintoshes to the Cornell community. Students purchased at least half of these machines. IBM PCs and compatibles, though not as popular with students, were also in heavy demand. The emergence of sophisticated spreadsheets and database management software made the PC popular in departmental and administrative offices. In many cases, administrators saw the general-purpose microcomputer as a more versatile replacement for leased or aging word processors and dedicated mainframe terminals.

In addition to the several hundred microcomputers installed in campus computing facilities, thousands of the machines appeared in offices, laboratories, dormitory rooms, and apartments. This development has already changed the way that faculty members and students do their work at Cornell and will have an increasingly profound impact over the next several years, as communication networks improve across campus and begin to link the microcomputers.

THE BROADENING CIRCLE OF INSTRUCTION IN COMPUTING

There can be no question that computing plays a different and more pervasive role in the Cornell curriculum than it did five years ago. It is interesting to note, nevertheless, that this does not mean that enrollment in courses of the Department of Computer Science has jumped remarkably. The number of students taking Computer Science courses did increase 45 percent between 1980-81 and 1982-83, from 2,423 to 3,521, but enrollment steadied at that level and then actually dropped during 1984-85 to 3,364. Enrollment in Computer Science 100, Cornell's introductory programming course, also dropped slightly from a peak figure of 1,297 in the academic year 1982-83 to 1,278 during 1984-85.

Five years ago, the Department of Computer Science provided almost all the instruction in computing that took place at Cornell. This instruction occurred within the regular curriculum and treated computing as a formal academic discipline. Now, numerous academic departments teach or employ computing in one form or another in dozens of courses that are often not affiliated with the Department of Computer Science.

This trend is particularly apparent within Mann Library's constituent colleges. For example, the College of Agriculture, working in conjunction with the Department of Computer Science, established a course in 1983 that introduces students to microcomputers and applications software and covers some elementary programming concepts. A highly popular course in the Department of Education (within the College of Agriculture) offers three modules of microcomputer-centered instruction designed to expose students to the use of computers in education. The departments of Agricultural Economics and Agricultural Engineering established courses that made almost weekly use of microcomputers for financial analysis and the solution of problems in engineering. A number of courses in the College of Human Ecology require that students learn to search online databases and then use this skill to gather research materials for term projects. By the fall semester of 1985 as many as 30 courses in Mann's client colleges required occasional use of the computer for the completion of assignments.

Another area of rapid increase in computing activity was that of instructional workshops, which do not carry credit and thus stand outside the formal curriculum. Although Cornell Computer Services has consistently provided instructional services for at least the past five years, the nature of its offerings has changed dramatically since the introduction of microcomputers. During fall semester 1983, for instance, CCS offered approximately 100 workshops, of which two concerned the TERAK microcomputer. Most of the remainder of the sessions treated the Cornell mainframe computers and the software running on them. Over the course of the fall semester 1985, by contrast, CCS taught some 85 workshops in microcomputers and micro-computer-based applications software open to the university community, and fewer than 50 in the use of the university mainframes.

THE DECENTRALIZATION OF COMPUTING SUPPORT

Five years ago, the great majority of computing personnel at Cornell were employed by the university computing center--Cornell Computer Services. Now many of the colleges, together with units such as Personnel Services, have people on their staffs whose main work consists of computer support or training. This trend is supported by university administration, which is not eager to fund additional large increases in centralized support for computing.

On the administrative side of university operations, the two central business offices have dedicated computer staff. Several colleges have their own systems staff and operate their own minicomputers. In addition, the libraries and many academic departments employ programmers and systems analysts. Thus, where Computer Services once conducted all computer activity, it is now the center that holds together a large number of "nodes" of computer activity spread across the campus. Computer Services still runs and maintains the mainframe computers, still creates programs for administrative use, and still offers instruction in how to employ the variety of computing resources at Cornell to best advantage. Computer Services markets and services microcomputer hardware. Nevertheless, the role of Computer Services is changing. More and more, it is the technical and support resource to staff in the outer nodes who actually teach users computing and administer public facilities, and who are employed by the colleges, the libraries, and other organizations.

With the opening of the Microcomputer Center in 1984, Mann Library became one of these computing nodes, and, as a public-access facility, now ranks among the most visible focal points of computing at Cornell. In addition to providing access to microcomputers for our patrons, we have a large software collection that is integrated into the general collections of the library. We also conduct a program of instruction in the use of the microcomputer as a tool that allows one to locate, retrieve, and control information. Specifically, we teach the searching of online databases, the management of reprint files with a microcomputer, and selected applications software packages. Although we have by no means abandoned bibliographic instruction in the selection and use of traditional print sources, the facilities of the Microcomputer Center have allowed the library to broaden its offerings to include the control of information with a computer. Our goal is to provide patrons with a comprehensive program of "information literacy" that is integrated into the curricula of our client colleges.

As a new focal point for computing located within the library and administered by the library, the Microcomputer Center has fostered a strong relationship between Mann Library and Cornell Computer Services. We have cooperated with CCS for two years in programs of microcomputer instruction for faculty members, we support their workshop program with our microcomputer-equipped classroom, and we offer consulting services to the Cornell community in computing and information access which increasingly complement those of Computer Services. At this writing, we are working with CCS to produce what will serve in effect as a union catalog of software holdings at Cornell. This close relationship between Cornell Computer Services and the university libraries will grow vital to both organizations as the libraries more fully automate their operations and tools of access.

The chapters that follow treat the three major programmatic elements of our Microcomputer Center--the design and management of a public-access facility equipped with microcomputers (Part 1), the development and control of a software collection (Part 2), and the provision of instruction in information literacy to library patrons (Part 3). In a broader sense, we present a case to the library community--that microcomputer technology is growing so basic to the provision of access to and control over scholarly information that academic libraries must undertake to master, employ, and teach this technology as it applies to information.

Part 1

Providing Access to Microcomputers:

A Microcomputer Center

Chapter 1

Planning, Design, and Staffing

Howard Curtis

An academic library planning a public-access computer center must first determine the scope of its ambitions. Will the facility be located in the library merely for the convenience of students and faculty members, or will it play a major role in building the instructional programs, the services, and the collections of the library itself? The Microcomputer Center was built because we believe microcomputer technology will prove central to future forms of information retrieval, storage, and control. The Microcomputer Center is thus a library computer facility and not just a computer facility that happens to be located in a library. Every decision we have made stems from this distinction.

In 1982, the library Director established the automation of the library and the full exploitation of computer technology as major administrative goals. The Public Services Department began revising its methods of operation, with emphasis on improved services to research faculty and the provision of sophisticated online capabilities. During the summer of 1982, Public Services introduced a "Quicksearch" service, designed to make inexpensive database searching available to undergraduates. By mid-1983 the department had undertaken a large end-user training program in online searching for undergraduates, graduate students, and faculty, but was hampered by inadequate equipment (in the beginning, a pair of portable Texas Instruments terminals). In addition, as outlined in the Introduction, it had grown obvious that academic computing at Cornell was moving rapidly to the microcomputer, and that many students would purchase their own computers.

The chance to build a public-access microcomputer center in Mann Library came in the summer of 1983. Although the project represented a major commitment for the library, the decision to proceed, given the direction of library programs, was a necessary one. If money had not suddenly become available to build the Microcomputer Center, the library would have tried to secure funding through the budget process.

COLLEGE POLITICS—AN OPPORTUNITY

Several elements came together to make a microcomputer facility at Mann Library possible. First, the library's two supporting colleges, the College of Agriculture and Life Sciences and the College of Human Ecology, were planning active computer and information literacy programs that would require dedicated computer facilities. Despite a general shortage of space in the colleges, the library was fortunate enough to have available a large, underutilized room called the "Informal Study." Finally, as a result of a conscious hiring policy, the library had on its staff people with microcomputer skills who could plan some of the technical aspects of the new Microcomputer Center. Though these components--projected need, budget, space, and staff--are requirements for any successful project, the cost of a computer facility is particularly high in each of these areas.

Laying the groundwork for the Microcomputer Center had two important aspects. The first involved seeking and securing the understanding of interested faculty members, the support of administration, and the funds to construct the center. The second consisted of developing and writing up detailed plans for our proposed computer facility.

For at least five years before we established the Microcomputer Center, the Colleges of Agriculture and Human Ecology had sought to enhance the resources available for academic computing at Cornell and to increase their own independence as users of computing. In the late 1970s, when virtually all Cornell computing took place on the university mainframes, Mann's sponsoring colleges had funded a computing support staff--the Computing Activities Group (CAG)--that stood outside Cornell's central organization for computing, Cornell Computer Services. Although CAG was soon disbanded--a casualty of the intrinsically centralized nature of mainframe computing--the colleges continued to feel that they should exercise more control over their own computing resources. With the appearance of microcomputers in the early 1980s, pressures grew to provide interested faculty members with the machines, and to make computing more easily available to students.

Beginning in 1981, a series of faculty committees convened to consider what role the colleges should adopt in furthering the understanding and use of computing among faculty and students. The committees all recommended, in their turn, that college administration establish and staff their own computer centers to supplement the facilities available through Cornell Computer Services, and to ensure that the colleges could pursue their own programs. A start was made with the placement of 16 Apple II computers in a room for course use in Agriculture in 1981, but there was little movement in the two years that followed.

In the spring of 1983, a college advisory committee called the "Ad Hoc Committee on Instructional Computing" was formed. Though Mann Library was not initially represented on the Ad Hoc Committee, we succeeded in convincing college administration that excluding the library from such an enterprise was a serious oversight. From the beginning, the membership of the committee felt that the colleges should establish facilities equipped with microcomputers. Soon the question became where to place these computer clusters.

Naturally, Mann staff argued that one of the new centers should be placed in the library. We pointed out that a microcomputer facility would require a software collection to achieve its potential, and that the library was uniquely equipped to support and control such a collection; that access to microcomputers would allow us to further develop the program in end-user searching which the library had already undertaken; and that, given the increasing importance of online databases to academic research, public-access microcomputers would in either case soon be a necessity within the library.

The committee recommended that microcomputer facilities should be located in the departments of Agricultural Economics and Agricultural Engineering--the two most powerful users of computing within the College of Agriculture--and in the library. In addition, the College of Human Ecology was considering the possibility of a microcomputer center to supplement an existing mainframe computer facility in the college. Although this represented a political victory of sorts for Mann, it was much more an acknowledgment on the part of the committee that microcomputing was just as important to the future of the library's programs and to the fulfillment of its mission as it was to the teaching needs of the academic departments. In this sense, we had succeeded in educating the faculty about the needs of a modern research library.

THE INITIAL PLANNING PROCESS

The library began the detailed definition of what form its computing facility would assume even before the administrations of the colleges had formally accepted the recommendations of the Ad Hoc Committee. The first step was to involve a faculty member who had sat on the Ad Hoc Committee and also served on the earlier college computing committees. Known for his vocal support of computing facilities in the colleges and his somewhat cynical assessment of administration's willingness to meet this need, the professor proved a valuable consultant and ally, adding a subtle edge to the library's case.

The library submitted an eight-page memorandum describing its plans for the Informal Study in June 1983 and a full report in early August. The preparation of these documents included discussions with faculty members, an examination of existing terminal and microcomputer facilities operated by Cornell Computer Services, and a trip to see a microcomputer installation in the Learning Resources Center of the library at SUNY Cobleskill. Although these exercises were instructive, the central activity in planning the Microcomputer Center was the identification, through discussions among key members on the library staff, of the programs that the center would ultimately support. These programmatic considerations in turn dictated the physical environment of the center, as follows:

1. The library planned to expand its instructional program in the searching of online databases and to offer workshops in the use of microcomputers and applications software. It was also committed to making the new Microcomputer Center available for classes taught by college faculty and Cooperative Extension staff. This meant that the facility must include a classroom equipped with microcomputers and projection devices.

2. The library would begin to build a collection of microcomputer software and data files on diskette for use in the center. This dictated the provision of shelving and cabinet storage, the inclusion of a loan counter, and the choice of microcomputers with a market base broad enough to attract the production of commercial software for a period of years.

3. The library intended to support its end-user searching program in the Microcomputer Center, making necessary a number of telephone lines and modems. It was also desirable to link the facility to Cornell's broadband communications network at the earliest opportunity, to make available the resources of the university mainframes. We also anticipated making use of the Microcomputer Center to teach patrons the online catalog, which would require access to the mainframe computers.

4. An obvious conflict existed between the support of instruction in a "classroom," and the provision of access to a collection of microcomputer software and to online databases. What would patrons do when the facility was reserved for group instruction? Because the software collection, a number of the machines in the center, and communications facilities should be available even when the classroom was in use, we decided to limit the classroom to a portion of the Microcomputer Center's overall area.

5. The library needed new personnel to operate the Microcomputer Center and support its programs. We would thus have to provide office or work space for full-time and student employees.

This focus on programmatic goals allowed us to devise a floor plan and a proposal for equipping the Microcomputer Center which has worked well in practice. The draft version of the planning document was distributed to interested college faculty members, administrators, staff of the Cornell Cooperative Extension, and to Cornell Computer Services. Criticism was solicited and, in several cases, incorporated into the planning process. By the end of August 1983, Mann had approval from college administration to install a microcomputer facility on the first floor of the library. This began six months of design work and construction.

DESIGN AND CONSTRUCTION

The conversion of the old Informal Study into a Microcomputer Center was no small undertaking. Construction crews had to install air-conditioning equipment in a neighboring machinery room; drive a three-foot-square hole through 18 inches of concrete to connect the two rooms; wire the new Microcomputer Center for power, telephone, and data communications; erect office walls and paint existing walls; and install duct work, a new system of overhead lighting, a folding partition, and a dropped ceiling. In addition, the library had to arrange for the design and fabrication of computer furniture, shelving, and a loan counter; select and purchase office furniture, computer hardware, and computer peripherals; and assemble the beginnings of a collection of software.

Before any of this could begin, we had to track down the professor emeritus who owned a large and weighty collection of fossils stored in the machinery room and persuade him to consent to its removal. In this case, geological history kindly deferred to the coming of the new technology.

The complexity of the Microcomputer Center project called for the involvement of many people outside the staff of the library. The office of the Statutory Facility Coordinator at Cornell handled relations with contractors, construction bidding procedures, and much of the construction scheduling. Facilities Engineering, an enterprise unit of the university that does contract work for colleges and departments, planned the air-conditioning, electrical, and lighting systems, and worked closely with the vendors who performed the installations. The library, for its part, provided overall coordination and arranged for the purchase and installation of all furniture, carpeting, draperies, shelving, counters, microcomputers and peripheral equipment, computer supplies, and the contents of the start-up collection of software.

Lighting, electrical service, and carpeting have an important effect on the work environment in a computer facility. Lenses are now available for standard fluorescent fixtures which diffuse overhead light. Adding them controls glare in a computer center and eliminates the need for recessed lighting. We chose to provide electricity for our microcomputers with an undercarpet wiring system. This reduces the number of ugly exposed wires in a facility and permits adjustments in the wiring scheme should the library choose to change the floor plan in the future. The floor wiring was covered with 18-inch-square carpet tiles. Purchasing extra carpet tiles at installation time allows the library to maintain the appearance of the facility by replacing worn sections of carpeting.

The electrical power source in a computer facility should be protected against power "surges." Surge protectors can be installed at each workstation, but this capability is best provided at a central electrical panel for the facility as a whole. Static electricity is another problem that a library can counter in the planning stage. The extra cost of carpet designed to prevent the buildup of a static charge is well worth the protection it buys. Talk about "budget constraints" seldom consoles a patron who has lost data.

For furniture, the library identified a local firm with carpentry and cabinet-making skills that was interested in constructing custom-designed computer furniture. The intent was twofold: to provide computer tables and a loan counter of nonstandard size to fit the dimensions of the Informal Study, and to suggest in the Microcomputer Center the original Art Deco motif of the library building. The library worked with the vendor in designing the furniture and reviewed a prototype computer table before construction went ahead. Though more time consuming than a bulk purchase from a catalog, this effort resulted in a more pleasing and practical work environment than we could otherwise have achieved.

In selecting furniture and devising a floor plan for a microcomputer facility, planners must consider the needs and habits of the student computer user. Patrons do view their work on the computer monitor, but typically they need to refer at the same time to three pieces of paper, a pile of note cards, and an open textbook. Sufficient open work space is essential. Planners should not assume that students will sit upright at a computer, quiet and dutiful, for hours at a stretch. They will sprawl, tilt their chairs precariously back, or assume the lotus posture on the seats. Chairs must be rugged and well balanced. Wide aisles and elbow room are in order. The designers must allow not only for the seated patron but also for the irritated patron haranguing the printer, the hurried patron racing to a workstation to finish the last pages of a paper due in an hour, and the three patrons at one machine in a corner, gesticulating as they admire a tutorial program with splendid graphics.

EQUIPMENT DECISIONS

The purchasing decisions on microcomputers and other hardware were critical, both to the project budget and to the subsequent operation of the Microcomputer Center. Several factors influenced our thinking on the computers. First, as mentioned in the Introduction, for some months before we began our planning, Cornell Computer Services had offered to members of the Cornell community "deep discounts" on the IBM PC, the DEC Rainbow, and the new Apple Macintosh. This offer worked to narrow campus purchases rapidly to these three machines. Although the Computer Science Department had decided to move its introductory programming courses to the Macintosh, several faculty members in the library's sponsoring colleges who teach large computer courses were planning to use the IBM PC. Given the mission of Mann Library, the latter was the more immediate concern.

The deciding criterion, however, was the software library. The library staff had determined that a software collection would play a central role in the Microcomputer Center, and this decision dictated that we equip the facility with a computer we could be sure would attract the efforts of software developers for the longest possible time. In September 1983, the only reasonable choice was the IBM PC or a hardware compatible device, and at that time none of the manufacturers of compatibles was reliable.

The library staff thus decided to base the facility on the IBM PC but to provide some DEC Rainbows and Apple Macintoshes, so that we could run most of the software that would be of interest at Cornell. We also purchased several add-on boards that permit the IBM PC to run software written for the Apple II and for the CP/M operating system.

Printers presented a different problem. Providing a printer for every machine in the classroom end of the facility would reduce the number of microcomputers in the classroom. It would also deny patrons adequate table space at their workstations throughout the facility. Instead, the library decided to purchase switches, so that approximately half of the microcomputers in the facility could gain access to one of nine printers.

In practice, this arrangement has had the desirable effect of making patrons think before they print, saving equipment wear and paper. Still, in retrospect we believe that it is not well advised to establish microcomputer stations that do not have direct access to a printer. We have recently acquired funding for printers that will give each cluster of three microcomputers in the classroom access to a printer.

The noise generated by dot-matrix printers has also proven an occasional irritation. A possible solution to both problems, given current technology, would be to network all microcomputers in a public-access facility and then provide printing capabilities through the network. While this would allow the printer or printers to be physically isolated from the staff and student work areas, it would increase traffic, as patrons would frequently get up to fetch a printout. An alternative would be the quieter printers that have recently appeared on the market. Our experience suggests that acoustical enclosures will prove unacceptable in a public facility if they limit patron access to the printers.

Our Microcomputer Center began operation with only dot-matrix printers. Students interested in word processing lobbied intensively for a letter-quality printer and the library eventually relented and installed a laser printer. Unless a library is prepared to outlaw word processing, thus eliminating one of the most useful applications of a microcomputer in an academic setting, this issue will surely present itself.

THE FINAL LAYOUT

When it opened in April 1984, the Microcomputer Center contained 33 microcomputers for public access (29 IBM PCs, two DEC Rainbows, and two Apple Macintoshes) and three IBM PCs for staff use. We have since added two more Macintoshes because of student demand for that machine. The folding partition, which is well soundproofed, allows us to isolate 21 of the IBM PCs in a classroom setting. In addition to computers, the classroom is equipped with a video projector, so that workshop participants can observe what is taking place on the screen of the instructor's computer, a "liquid chalk" board, telecommunications connections, and seating to accommodate a group of up to 40.

The folding partition is left open when the classroom is not in use for group instruction, making the Microcomputer Center one large, open room. When the classroom is occupied, the 14 public-access microcomputers nearest the entrance to the center remain available to walk-in patrons. This "general use" portion of the Microcomputer Center contains the Macintosh and DEC microcomputers, as well as eight IBM PCs, the laser printer, four machines with color graphics capabilities, telecommunications connections, and the software library. While waiting times may increase when the classroom is in use, group instruction does not deny patrons access to any of the center's services.

The northern end of the Microcomputer Center contains the software circulation desk, and behind it what our student assistants call the "Operator's Lair." This area contains two microcomputers--one to run the program that controls software circulation and patron use of the center's microcomputers and one for general staff work--the software collection, reference materials, and the student assistant's desk and work area. Next to the Lair is a small office occupied by the Microcomputer Center Manager.

THE "ONLINE CLASSROOM"

Within six months of the opening of the Microcomputer Center, the library staff had to plan for the expansion of its microcomputer facilities. As just noted, use of the classroom in the Microcomputer Center for group instruction reduces the number of computers available to walk-in patrons from 35 to 14. While we consider this unavoidable when the participants in a classroom session need microcomputers for hands-on training, about 40 percent of the workshops held in the classroom during our first nine months of operation involved only an instructor's presentation and a demonstration on screen of an online search or a microcomputer software package. At these times, 21 machines were unavailable though only one was required, while patrons waited in frustration for computers in the "general-use" end of the Microcomputer Center.

The "Online Classroom," which opened in May 1985, alleviates this problem. This new facility, located down the hall from the Microcomputer Center, contains two computers, a video projector, communications connections, and tables and chairs for 30 people. All instruction that does not involve hands-on training now takes place in the Online Classroom.

SERVICES THE CENTER PROVIDES

The Microcomputer Center offers library patrons access to an extensive software collection and an opportunity to use the IBM PCs, DEC Rainbow 100s, and Apple Macintosh computers described above. Patrons can use dot-matrix printers, for which we do not charge, and a letter-quality laser printer. The two full-time staff members and 25 student employees provide consulting support on questions and problems related to the center's software collection and the operation of its hardware devices. The library offers formal instructional sessions in microcomputer software packages and information-related applications. The staff of the Microcomputer Center and the library's

Public Services Department maintain a working expertise in bibliographic management software, gateway systems to online databases, and expert systems. We offer consulting services to faculty in these areas. These services and programs are described in detail in the chapters that follow.

STAFFING CONSIDERATIONS

Mann Library recognized from the start that without new staff members we could not support a microcomputer facility and the full spectrum of programs that we proposed. The written proposal to college administration defined two full-time positions. The first was a mid-level professional position, ultimately assigned the title "Computer Projects Coordinator." This individual was to be responsible for the overall management of the Microcomputer Center; for structuring, administering, and participating in a program of workshops in microcomputer applications; for training and supporting library staff in the use of microcomputers in their work; for general library automation planning and budget preparation; for representing the library in computer-related forums; and for some collection development activity in the area of software.

The second position had a high-level support staff ranking and was initially given a university job title of "Computer Operator," because of the technical skills required. The library later adopted the working title "Microcomputer Center Manager," however, as a more appropriate description of the position and its responsibilities. This person manages the Microcomputer Center on a day-to-day basis, supervises student employees, coordinates the maintenance and repair of computer equipment, teaches workshops, and helps support library staff projects that involve microcomputers.

Library personnel also realized early in the planning process that these full-time employees would require the support of a staff of student assistants. With an extensive software collection and a loan counter, we were proposing nothing less than the installation of an additional public service point in the library. The hardware in the Microcomputer Center would be valuable and delicate; its use would have to be monitored. Loans from the software collection would generate desk work. Staff members anticipated as well that patrons would have questions about the behavior of our microcomputers and software packages, although we did not learn until later how extensive the consulting role would become.

We originally estimated that the library would require 89 hours of work by student assistants per week during the Cornell academic semesters. In practice, our need for student assistants had reached approximately 150 hours per week by the height of the spring semester 1985. During peak evening hours, one student was occupied almost constantly handling loan transactions and routine chores. It was only with a second student assistant on duty that the Microcomputer Center was able to respond in any way to patron demand for consulting support, which may well be the most valuable service that the center offers its student clientele. (The selection, training, and management of our student staff is covered in Chapter 2.)

ORGANIZATIONAL IMPLICATIONS

Any library that installs a public-access microcomputer center must decide where to place the staff of the new unit in its overall organizational structure. One obvious possibility, in that a microcomputer facility serves library patrons directly, is to incorporate the staff of the computer facility into the library's Public Services department. Mann Library decided to structure things differently, however, and this decision speaks to our conception of the broader role of the Microcomputer Center within the organization. The full-time staff members of the Microcomputer Center now constitute the "Information Technology Section," a unit of the Administrative Department. The head of the section reports directly to the director of the library. The staff of the Information Technology Section, in addition to their duties in operating the Microcomputer Center, encourage the introduction of microcomputer technology throughout the library, train staff members to use computing in their work, and play an important role in planning for library automation. When time allows, the ITS also undertakes research projects, usually in conjunction with Public Services, into the potential of emerging information storage and retrieval technologies. The Information Technology Section thus supports both Public Services and Technical Services, and is best viewed as an administrative service to the entire library.

Although the operation of the Microcomputer Center and the conduct of its instructional program for students and faculty members in the application of microcomputers currently consumes approximately 70 percent of the time of the staff of the Information Technology Section, this is beginning to change. As the operations of the Microcomputer Center stabilize, the administrative burden of establishing a complex new program will lessen. Student employees will assume more responsibility for the routine operation of the center. In addition, the library has currently secured the funding to add at least one more professional position to the staff of the Information Technology Section as we proceed toward fully automated operations. It is thus likely that within a year the ITS will dedicate more time to staff support, library automation activities, and the exploration of emerging computing technologies than it does to the operation of the Microcomputer Center itself.

ASKING THE RIGHT QUESTIONS

As outlined above, good planning for a public-access microcomputer facility in an academic library begins with an examination of the programs the center will support. This clarification of programmatic goals allows the library to contend with the multitude of questions that must be addressed in creating a computer facility.

Because a library's own programs should dictate the design of a library microcomputer facility, we do not believe that Mann Library, or anyone else, has a model that may be peddled as the answer to everyone's needs. Nevertheless, given the present state of microcomputer technology (in constant flux, but headed toward workstations linked by local area networks that support highly capable mass-storage devices, including compact and optical disk readers), the state of the software industry (a brier patch of inconsistency, quasi-legal restriction, and technical complexity, from the library point of view that, for better or worse, will play a large role in the future of information transfer and control), and the role of the library within the university, certain questions will present themselves to almost any library that seeks to install a microcomputer center. Among these, the following points merit particular attention:

1. Who will fund the library's microcomputer facility? Are they persuaded that the library needs such a facility? If not, how can the library present its case most effectively (representation on committees or other forums, contacts with administration, the preparation of a detailed report)? Does the funding organization know the real costs of installing the kind of facility that the library wants? Has the library made an accurate estimate of these costs?

2. Will the library or other parties use the microcomputer facility for group instruction? Who will constitute the primary audiences for this instruction? Will the participants in instructional sessions need to have a

computer in front of them, or will projection on a screen at the front of a classroom be adequate?

3. What types of software are required to support the instructional programs planned? What will it cost to provide the necessary packages in sufficient numbers? Are these costs included in the project budget?

4. Will the microcomputer facility support a full software collection? If so, will use of the software be limited to the premises of the facility, or does the library wish to support (and negotiate with vendors) out-of-the-building loans? Will the library conduct software circulation from an existing circulation point or create a new one? Where will the software be stored? Who will maintain the software collection? Will technical services fully catalog the software? If so, will a professional cataloger take this task on as a new responsibility? If the library plans to collect software on a continuing basis, will the money come from existing acquisitions funds or a new source?

5. Will the library provide access to online databases in the microcomputer center?

6. What communications connections and hardware will be necessary to support the instructional program and online services that take place in the computer facility?

7. Should some or all of the microcomputers in the new facility be networked? What services will this network provide? Does the installation of a network have implications for software loan activity, the placement of printers in the facility, or the instructional program?

8. Can the library absorb the new activities without additional personnel? If new positions are required, who will fund them? Where will the new staff fit into the library's present organization? What will be the relationship of the library computing personnel with the university or college academic computing establishment? Will part-time or student assistants also be needed?

9. What will be the relationship between the microcomputer facility and other computer-based activities in the library (microcomputers for staff use, an existing or planned local online system, database search services, and so on)?

This list of questions presupposes that the library will administer the microcomputer facility, and that the staff of the facility will report to the administration of the library. In the alternative model, wherein the library makes space available for a facility administered by the campus computing agency, library administration ultimately has little to say about the purposes to which the computers are put. This statement is not made to advocate a power struggle between the library and the academic computing organization.

In fact, with the introduction of online catalogs and the progressive automation of information storage and transfer in general, the need for close cooperation between these two agencies on most campuses is compelling. Until the library is in a position to support its own programs with computers, however, and has personnel with a solid understanding of computer technology, it may not be able to define creatively what the purpose and the nature of this cooperation should be.

SUMMARY

1. The pressure to provide increased academic computing resources on most campuses is such that if a library pursues the proper administrative channel, it may well be able to trade space for the kind of microcomputer facilities and staffing that it needs to upgrade its programs of instruction and online access.

2. Before planning the details of a public-access microcomputer center, a library should define how the facility will support its goals and programs. The library should insure that a microcomputer center will help further its basic mission--to provide patrons with access to information, and to train them in how that information is best located, retrieved, and controlled. The design of the microcomputer facility--floor plan, equipment configuration, staffing, and so on--should derive from the library's programmatic goals.

3. Planning and installing a large microcomputer facility is a complex project. Library administration should anticipate involving staff members from other units of the college or university, including, perhaps, the computing center and facilities management.

4. The potential conflict between "walk-in" use of a microcomputer center and group instruction is one that deserves careful thought in the planning process. If group instruction is allowed to fully occupy the facility, at certain times patrons will be denied access to other services that the library may wish to offer.

5. Operating a public-access microcomputer facility of any size is a major undertaking for a library. It revolves around a complex technology that still frustrates many users. Adequate staffing to support the new facility is a primary consideration. Comparisons with existing audiovisual facilities may well prove deceptive.

6. A library should carefully consider how to incorporate any new, computer-related staff into its organizational structure. Is the role of this staff a public services function or an administrative service to the entire library?

7. Public-access microcomputers in the library provide an excellent vehicle for forming closer ties with the academic computing establishment on campus. This relationship will be critical to both organizations in the coming years, as the provision of high-quality access to scholarly information becomes increasingly dependent on computing and communications technologies.

Chapter 2

Policy Considerations and Day-to-Day Operations

James Madden

The Mann Library Microcomputer Center serves two functions. Its primary function is that of a sophisticated information resource. Through the library's training program in online searching and the search stations that the Microcomputer Center provides, users may access information critical to their research. The center also offers the university community an opportunity to explore software packages and data files. As a secondary function, the Microcomputer Center serves as a classroom facility. The center supports both library instructional programs, explained in detail in Part 3, and various College courses that include a component of hands-on computer training and, possibly, follow-up assignments.

The dual nature of the Microcomputer Center--information resource and classroom facility--has posed a dilemma for the library. As noted in the Introduction, the Microcomputer Center is now one of at least six computer facilities at Cornell established with college, as opposed to university, funds. Others of these computer centers limit access to students and faculty members of the funding college. Since our Microcomputer Center is a unit of a university library system providing information services, we felt it imperative that the entire university community be allowed access. This principle has always operated with books in the collections of the various libraries at Cornell, no matter which college was the funding source. We wanted to make it clear that the same principle must apply to online resources and other sources of information in machine-readable form.

Library administrators could not politically afford to be so broad-minded, however, when it came to the Microcomputer Center's computer classrooms. The individual colleges at Cornell have traditionally controlled and scheduled their own classrooms. In addition, they charge each other for access to facilities fitted with expensive equipment. As our two microcomputer-equipped classrooms are highly visible and attractive, the library had to avoid compromising the interests of its two sponsoring colleges in this area.

In addition to meeting our responsibilities to the College of Agriculture and the College of Human Ecology, we wanted to insure that college courses which were essentially "computer courses" in content did not monopolize our new instructional facilities. Our goal was to support an active program of library instruction in the retrieval and control of information and to encourage the spread of computing within the curricula of the colleges to courses that had not employed computing in the past.

The rules that regulate use of the Microcomputer Center and the Online Classroom reflect this set of concerns. Library policies govern access to hardware, access to the classroom, software usage, costs to users, and other issues. It has been necessary to modify these policies and to adapt them to unanticipated situations on occasion, but the staff time the library dedicated to establishing policies before the Microcomputer Center opened has proven a wise investment. Access to computers remains a scarce resource at Cornell, as at most universities. A library that operates a microcomputer center must contrive to regulate usage in a manner that is just but that also preserves the integrity of the library's programs.

ACCESS TO THE MICROCOMPUTER CENTER'S COMPUTERS

The first set of policy issues the library addressed was hardware access. The questions we faced included who might use the facility, how much time should be allowed for a work session, whether we would allow patrons to reserve equipment, and whether we would loan computer hardware.

Our view that the Microcomputer Center constitutes a library information resource, as outlined above, dictated our position on the use of the computers and software library by walk-in patrons. Since, in the interests of free inquiry, a library must not limit information access to selected constituencies within the university, the Microcomputer Center is open to the entire Cornell community.

Users must present a valid ID card at the start of each work session. This we hold until they have finished their work and returned all software. Only one computer may be assigned to each ID card holder. Children are welcome, but only so long as they are accompanied by the holder of a valid ID throughout their work session. This provision has saved the Microcomputer Center from doubling as a high-tech day-care center.

In order to provide equitable access to equipment and software, the library restricts patrons to one hour per work session when people are waiting.

A queuing program running on the microcomputer located on the loan counter records check-in times and software circulation transactions. Patrons frequently prefer to work for periods much longer than one hour and are welcome to do so, provided another patron is not waiting to use a workstation. When there is a queue, we ask patrons who have been working for the longest time in excess of an hour to surrender their stations.

The Microcomputer Center assigns computers on a first-come-first-served basis. With the exception of one station for letter-quality printing, patrons may not reserve the machines in the facility in advance. People are allowed to sign up for a maximum of two half-hour slots on the high-quality print station each week. Available printing blocks are often claimed several days in advance.

The 21 workstations in the classroom section of the Microcomputer Center are often not available for general use during the week because of classes and workshops. Staff members of the Microcomputer Center post a schedule of classroom activities for the following week every Friday to assist patrons in planning their own work schedules. In devising policies for the facility, we decided that no classroom activities would be scheduled after 8:00 in the evening. We thus guarantee patrons maximum access to computers from 8:00 to 12:00 in the evenings, as well as on Saturdays and Sundays. The construction of the Online Classroom, described in Chapter 1, has also served to increase the availability of machines to walk-in patrons.

During our first month of operation in the spring of 1984, some 1,300 patrons visited the Microcomputer Center. By the end of the spring semester 1985, use was running at just less than 5,000 patrons per month, not including workshop attendance, and demand was still growing. Although several thousand students at Cornell have purchased personal computers in the last two years, the public-access machines in computer facilities around the campus continue to be in high demand. Students increasingly view access to a microcomputer, whether it be for programming, word processing, or information retrieval, as a requirement for academic success. Our one-hour time limit insures that everyone has a fair chance. To allow students to make the most profitable use of their time, the Microcomputer Center has recently installed a system of external monitors that broadcast to library study areas information concerning the queue of people waiting for machines. This addition will permit our patrons to work while they wait.

According to campus tradition, the stereotypical "hacker" always begins work in the late evening and performs best between midnight and dawn. These habits began in response to lags in mainframe processing time in the days of card readers, batch jobs, and operator intervention. In those early years the best turnaround time was to be had during off-peak hours. Computer users retained their late-night schedules after the introduction of interactive computing, and even now, though "response time" is the same in the morning and at midnight with a microcomputer, many people still prefer late hours because they encounter few interruptions and distractions.

Our library currently closes at midnight on week nights during the academic semester. Because of the preferences of computer users, administration has encountered some pressure to extend these hours. If the introduction of computing does force a library to lengthen its operating hours, of course, the opportunity exists to offer other library services as well. Although the center's hours may well be extended in the future, the present library administration will likely draw the line at canned food, camp stoves, and army cots.

Library planners considered the possibility of loaning computer hardware, but decided against it. This is certainly a legitimate activity for a library, but it was not essential to our goals for the Microcomputer Center. We needed microcomputer hardware in the library to support our instructional programs, a new software collection, and sophisticated information retrieval techniques. The hardware would function best in this capacity if it remained in place and under our control. The loaning of hardware, we decided, was a separate proposition, associated perhaps with a media center rather than with the microcomputer center we envisioned.

The center occasionally receives requests from academic departments to borrow equipment for various reasons. In order to guarantee fair access to all of the library's constituencies, however, we resist the temptation to help except when it is absolutely clear that our local users will not suffer inconvenience.

ACCESS TO THE MICROCOMPUTER CENTER CLASSROOMS

As suggested above, we do not believe that the principle of free access to information extends to the reservation of our classroom facilities for group instruction. When we planned the Microcomputer Center, it was clear that the classroom would be in great demand as computing spread in the Cornell curriculum. This caused us to think carefully about how we would regulate classroom use.

Before deciding who could use the classrooms, we considered the types of instructional activities the rooms would support. For instance, we conduct workshops and seminars that contain hands-on computer exercises in the Microcomputer Center classroom, while demonstrations take place in the neighboring Online Classroom. The Microcomputer Center classroom supports components of courses but is not available for weekly use throughout the semester by computer courses. Examples of course-related activities include a two-week project in designing spreadsheet templates to manage the operation of a greenhouse business undertaken by students in a Floriculture course, training in a word-processing package for students in a Communication Arts course who must then use the software to write their term papers, and an introduction to a BASIC program that simulates the growth of deer populations in a Natural Resources course. We effectively restrict course use to this kind of "component" activity by setting a limit of eight hours of access per course each semester. Finally, both the Microcomputer Center classroom and the Online Classroom support the library's own instructional programs, wherever these require the use of a microcomputer.

Because of the high demand for computer time in the Microcomputer Center, the Microcomputer Center Manager tries to insure that every group reserving the classroom in the center actually needs microcomputers for individual participants and will consist of at least 10 people. This minimizes complaints from walk-in patrons that the machines in the room next door are "going to waste."

After deciding the set of activities that could take place in the center, we took up the question of which groups would be admitted. Our mission as a library dictated that the departments of our sponsoring colleges, and the Cooperative Extension organizations affiliated with them, would be our principal users. In addition, library personnel would use the facility both to teach college audiences and to provide staff training. In the interests of cooperation among the units of the Cornell library system, we decided to make the classroom available to staff members of other libraries when demand from our primary audiences was not overwhelming. We also determined to admit groups such as the IBM PC Users Group at Cornell, whose activities provide benefits to students and faculty in all the university's colleges, on an occasional basis.

Cornell Computer Services, which conducts numerous instructional sessions in the use of microcomputers, also expressed an interest in using the classroom. The realities of college funding at Cornell would not normally have permitted such an arrangement. However, the library was able to use this political obstacle to arrive at a mutually beneficial agreement. We felt it was important that the library be connected to the campus data communications network, and within 18 months we would require such a connection to use the local integrated library system that is to be installed at Cornell. The library therefore arranged a trade with Cornell Computer Services whereby we provided a specified number of hours of classroom access per month in return for cabling and communications hardware. Depending on the institutional environment, there may be the potential for a library to secure some of its needs in computer hardware and computer-related services through such an arrangement.

Once our audiences were clear, we set scheduling lead times ranging from 60 to 120 days so that groups of highest priority would have an opportunity to schedule the room in advance of groups with a low priority. During the Microcomputer Center's first 15 months of operation, the classroom in the center was used 255 times for a total of 590 hours. In controlling this volume of activity, the clarity and completeness of our list of audiences by priority has more than compensated for the complexity of our ranking system.

SOFTWARE POLICIES

In establishing a collection of microcomputer software, library administrators must decide whether to limit use to machines within the building, or whether to circulate software packages like books. Relationships with software vendors, which we will take up in greater detail in Part 2, grow more difficult and complex if a library wishes to support out-of-the-building loans.

At Cornell, both types of software collections currently exist. Cornell Computer Services maintains a lending library from which patrons may borrow software for use on personal or office hardware. Before checking out the software, the borrower must leave a check or departmental account number as collateral, with the understanding that a fee of 125 percent of retail value will be assessed if the package is damaged or illegally copied. This arrangement gives Computer Services some leverage in persuading vendors to make their software packages available to the lending library.

Apart from the logistics of reserving an opportunity to preview a popular package and the frequent need to wait for the software to become available, this arrangement has worked reasonably well. One difficulty with out-of-the-building software loans, of course, is that the lender has no control over the hardware the patron will use. Unless the borrower is highly conversant with microcomputers, software configuration is often a problem.

At the library we decided to limit software circulation to the premises of the Microcomputer Center. There were three primary reasons: (1) we felt this would put us in a strong position in our efforts to convince vendors that we are serious about protecting their rights; (2) it is difficult to support software running on computer systems that are not under the direct control of the library; and (3) limiting use to the Microcomputer Center would assure patrons that they would not have to wait long to secure a particular package.

We take a strong and public position on the infringement of the rights of software vendors. For instance, a printed statement prohibiting the copying of commercial software appears at each workstation (see the Appendix). The logic of these policies is explored in greater detail in Chapter 5. Patrons may borrow software documentation as they would borrow other reserve materials from the library, that is, for a short-term loan. Documentation may be taken outside the building if the patron so chooses. Diskettes from all commercial packages, on the other hand, must remain in the Center at all times.

COSTS TO USERS

In those areas where the Microcomputer Center serves as an information resource, we seek to provide our services to all members of the Cornell community without direct charges. Patrons are not charged to use the software collection nor do they pay to use the microcomputers as an academic tool for organizing and processing information. By contrast, the library does not feel responsible for providing the media on which people take their work away from the facility. Users must bring their own storage diskettes if they wish to protect their work. The library does sell diskettes at the Circulation Desk as a convenience to patrons. Similarly, though the library provides access to a laser printer, we charge for this service by the page to cover our costs. This is consistent with our approach to the provision of photocopy services. Output on a dot-matrix printer is free to the patron.

Due to the high cost of online searches, the library must recover expenses in its searching program for end-users. When possible, we seek to make arrangements with the sponsoring college or department to subsidize student searches. In cases where such a mechanism does not exist the library charges the searcher directly. We believe that direct charges for a basic level of online information access are undesirable in an academic environment, particularly where the patron does not have access to grant funds, and are working to improve and rationalize our vehicles for cost recovery.

OTHER ISSSUES

Some policy issues required little or no discussion in the early planning stages of the Microcomputer Center. Eating, drinking, and smoking are strictly prohibited. While many users would like to nibble a donut or sip coffee at their workstations, the administration believes that strict enforcement of this policy is the only way to maintain the facility's appearance and the condition of software materials. Also, the lethal effects of coffee, cola, and chocolate on a microcomputer keyboard are well known.

Users are expected to be reasonably quiet, courteous to others, and to treat hardware and software as if it were their own. Occasionally Center personnel find it necessary to resolve a confrontation between users or to suggest that a frustrated patron take a break before he or she damages a piece of hardware. Fortunately, these occasions are relatively rare, and their incidence becomes less frequent as users grow more sophisticated and the mysteries surrounding the operation of a microcomputer are dispelled.

OPERATIONAL REQUIREMENTS

Users come to the Microcomputer Center with high expectations concerning the printout they would like to have in hand when they walk away. Often they fail to obtain expected results and experience great frustration. While it is not possible to eliminate user frustrations, the center staff attempts to make a patron's computing experience at the library as pleasant and productive as possible.

Student Support Staff

It would be difficult to overstate the value of the center's student support staff. The center has managed to hire and retain a group of talented and highly motivated students. Students are drawn to the position because it offers them an opportunity to learn about microcomputers and software applications, and to assist their fellow students in an area where they can boast a valuable expertise. Because the position is attractive, the Microcomputer Center can select from a large pool of applicants. Applicants complete a library-designed employment application form which asks them to describe their academic interests, their computer experience, related public service experience, interests and hobbies, and the personal qualities which, in their opinion, best qualify them for the position. While a student's application, in most cases, provides an accurate description of his or her qualifications, two full-time staff members of the Information Technology Section interview all applicants before choosing those who will join the center's staff.

When we first sought student employees to work in the Microcomputer Center, we decided to hire people with a wide variety of backgrounds and academic interests. Naturally, a few of the operators major in electrical engineering or computer science and have a solid knowledge of computer hardware. Several are "aggies" (students majoring in agriculture), giving them a subject background important to many among our clientele. Others major in nutritional sciences, history, physics, and a variety of other disciplines. A few of the center's student employees have technical repair skills, a number are gifted programmers, some have a thorough understanding of software packages such as Lotus or dBase III, or of the Macintosh computer. The students enjoy solving new problems or helping a user through a computer-related crisis. As academic computing, in the form of the microcomputer, reaches new campus audiences, diversity in the staff of a computer facility becomes increasingly beneficial.

As the quality of the Microcomputer Center depends to a large degree on the performance of our student staff, we stress training and systematic communications. New student operators receive about three hours of training before they assume their duties and then spend their first shift with a full-time staff member or an experienced fellow student. Meetings of all student operators on the center's staff take place at the beginning of each semester and at least once during the semester.

When students join the staff of the Microcomputer Center, they are expected to learn certain tasks and routines which are integral to the center's operation. They must be able to circulate software, assist with the basic operation of equipment in the center, develop a cursory understanding of the most popular software packages, and prepare themselves to field a wide variety of questions from patrons who encounter difficulties. Students must demonstrate a capacity to assume these responsibilities before they are asked to join the center's staff.

It is difficult to spend much time in the Microcomputer Center without absorbing large quantities of information about microcomputer software and the problems users encounter in mastering its operation. After several weeks spent learning "the ropes," student operators usually begin to acquire additional knowledge in areas which interest them. In our second semester of operation, we formalized this tendency by assigning fields of concentration to our student assistants. When the students have developed some expertise in a particular area of hardware or software, we can present them with projects to which they can apply their expertise.

Among other projects, students on the Microcomputer Center staff have developed a program to monitor activity in the Microcomputer Center, organized and updated the software collection, created Lotus templates to generate our statistical reports, kept statistics of the center's usage, produced a guide to operational procedures for the center's staff, and solved and documented hardware and software problems. Several students now serve as coaches in the library's online searching program, while others teach in our software workshops (see Part 3). Some students have elected to specialize in hardware maintenance.

Because there is always something new to learn or do in the world of microcomputing, the Microcomputer Center has an advantage in generating interest and maintaining enthusiasm among its student staff. Motivated students respond well to the challenge of a new assignment or an individual project. Most of the students appreciate a chance to apply some of the theoretical knowledge they have gained in their studies to a tangible situation in the workplace. They derive a sense of accomplishment from completing special assignments and are grateful for opportunities to extend their knowledge of computers and to become familiar with a new software package.

Used properly, students with computer skills can be a valuable resource to a library. We try to see that our student employees contribute to the library itself, and not just to the operation of Microcomputer Center. In addition to the Microcomputer Center projects mentioned above, we also assign students programming and software projects that will be of use to the staff of the library.

Working in a highly visible public facility has social benefits for student employees as well. Most student assistants enjoy meeting and assisting their peers. This is called "face-time" in Cornell jargon.

Operating Costs

The Microcomputer Center would not function well without adequate staffing. A great resource would remain untapped and a major investment in equipment and software would depreciate rapidly. In fact, the center's greatest operational expense is staffing. The library also spends a considerable sum on supplies, such as the paper, printer cartridges, and ribbons required for the daily operation of the center.

In addition to purchasing supplies that are consumed quickly in the course of normal operation, the library dedicates funds to maintaining its collection of software. Many software packages contain three or more floppy diskettes. From these diskettes we produce a set of circulating diskettes and, in most cases, a set of working master copies of the program diskettes. In other words, we use two new diskettes for each diskette acquired from a software vendor.

Commercial software rarely arrives in packaging designed for constant circulation. In order to preserve these materials and to prepare them for the type of circulation activity seen in the Microcomputer Center, we purchase special packaging materials from computer supply outlets. It is also necessary to anticipate fees for the binding of documentation. These issues will be addressed in greater detail in Chapters 6 and 7.

Charges for telephone and computer communications are another major area of expenditures. Staff members of the Microcomputer Center must frequently contact software and hardware vendors, resulting in substantial telephone bills. In addition, if a library proposes to subsidize patrons' costs for the searching of commercial databases, the potential Pandora's box of "online" charges opens.

Hardware Maintenance

There are several approaches to hardware maintenance. Most hardware is covered by warranties that run from 90 days to one year. The question is, what should the library do when these warranties expire? Maintenance contracts cost on average ten percent of the original purchase price of computer hardware and, in most cases, require that the supplier of the maintenance agreement provide all service. The high cost and limiting terms of this approach encouraged us to suggest to our funding colleges that we take, initially, a pay-as-you-go approach to the maintenance problem. This decision has resulted in substantial dollar savings over our first 18 months of operation. Electronic components and computer chips have only rarely failed. Our most common problem has been disk drive malfunction, which can be remedied by simply installing a new drive. It remains to be seen what will happen as the equipment grows older.

The student staff of the center performs routine maintenance, such as the cleaning of disk drives, screens, and printers. Likewise, many minor hardware problems can be diagnosed and resolved on-site, avoiding exorbitant maintenance fees. Because the library owns a large number of similar machines, it makes sense to train employees to handle routine problems. We stock supplies of certain computer components, such as memory chips, disk drives, and spare keyboards.

Occasionally, problems occur which cannot be handled on-site. Since the center is not tied to any particular service agency, the library is then free to select the vendor we feel will service a particular problem most competently and with the least downtime.

LOOKING AHEAD

The Microcomputer Center has now been open for portions of six academic semesters and two summer sessions. During that time, Cornell has seen many changes that affect the use of microcomputers in academic computing. There are new computer facilities at several locations around campus, equipped with microcomputers rather than dumb terminals. As noted in the Introduction, microcomputers are beginning to play a significant role in courses where computing is simply a tool of analysis, rather than the subject matter of the course. Nearly all students now encounter computers in their course work. In addition, many students have purchased their own machines.

As patron demand grows, we will need to define carefully where full-time staff members will play a consulting role and where we will depend entirely on our student employees. Given our budget constraints and the great wave of computer use that Cornell is experiencing, it is inevitable that student operators in the Microcomputer Center will provide technical support at a level that libraries have not entrusted to part-time staff in the past. Training student operators and properly utilizing their talents will be a major challenge during the next few years.

Future policy considerations will address alternative methods of supplying information to our patrons, as well as the role the library will play in the development of academic databases and the machines that provide access to them. Ideally the library will allow its patrons access to information wherever it may be stored. However, the policies which regulate the use of workstations and available network connections will require considerable thought. The library will give highest priority to computing activities that are related to obtaining information. The local management of electronic information will, of course, be allowed to the extent that our facilities can support such activities. The selection of online databases and the recovery of the costs incurred in maintaining connections to these sources of information are issues which must be addressed as the spectrum of online services offered continues to broaden.

The Microcomputer Center is already experiencing a traditional library problem--we are running out of storage and shelf space. We have now secured the funding to introduce a local area network which supports a substantial file-server in the Microcomputer Center. This installation will allow us to make our most popular software packages available "online" at each computer, reducing to some degree our storage requirements for the software collection and cutting the number of loan transactions conducted over the counter. A local area network will also offer protection against diskette wear and theft.

If we are to continue keeping the sort of circulation statistics that we currently produce, and that libraries are able to generate with an automated circulation system for print materials, the network software must have the capacity to record the number of times that each program file is downloaded to users' machines. In addition, if we are to continue to assure software vendors that we will not concurrently run more copies of a package than we have purchased, the network software should be able to impose limits on the number of machines allowed to run one program concurrently.

A local area network within the Microcomputer Center is, then, our next major technological step. We look forward to a day when patrons at any machine in the Microcomputer Center will have reasonable access not only to our local collections of microcomputer software but also to the mainframe computers at Cornell, to the library's online catalog, and, perhaps, to external databases and information resources.

SUMMARY

1. A microcomputer center is a highly visible resource that a library must manage carefully, both programmatically and politically, to insure that the library offers its constituencies equitable treatment and that it is able to further its own programs through the new facility.

2. A library that is committed to the use of microcomputers as tools of information access, retrieval, and management may decide to stress this aspect of microcomputing in administering its computer facility. Wherever information resources are at stake, library policies on the provision of access to microcomputers should parallel those for the print collections, in the interests of freedom of academic inquiry. On the other hand, a library may wish to more narrowly regulate access to a microcomputer classroom or "laboratory," in keeping with campus political considerations.

3. Software policies can be established on either of two basic premises--software will circulate only within the microcomputer center, or software may be taken from the facility and used on the patron's own machine.

We have chosen the former model. This choice will affect the library's relationship with software vendors and influence hardware requirements. It is difficult to configure software for out-of-the-building loans, and difficult to offer assistance to patrons who encounter problems working on office or home machines.

4. While the library assumes the costs of operating the Microcomputer Center and making information available to the public, patrons are expected to supply their own working materials, to pay for letter-quality output, and to reimburse the library for charges incurred while searching online commercial databases.

5. The Microcomputer Center is staffed throughout the week by student employees. These students can be an extremely valuable resource, both in patron support and in assisting with the automation of library functions, if they are carefully selected and managed. A library should give thought to the need for adequate student staffing before installing a microcomputer facility. Computer expertise is important in student employees, but people with communications skills and a range of academic backgrounds are also an asset.

6. In addition to staffing costs, a microcomputer center requires funding for supplies, the processing and support of the software collection, telecommunications, and hardware maintenance. In most cases, a large microcomputer center will save money by avoiding maintenance contracts and paying for hardware repairs as necessary. Nevertheless, the library must budget for this expense.

7. As libraries attempt to keep pace with technology, they can look forward to increasingly sophisticated, and potentially expensive, applications of microcomputers. The technology does offer innovative methods for accessing and retrieving information that libraries cannot ignore. We envision a day in the near future when all of our center's workstations will have access through a local area network to local software holdings, the campus mainframe computers, the library's online catalog, and external information resources.

Part 2

A Software Library

Chapter 3

Collection Policy

Katherine Chiang

Research libraries exist to collect, preserve, organize, and provide access to the information that serves the teaching and research needs of the university community. Software provides access to and control over information. In many cases, we would argue that software itself *is* information. For these reasons, research libraries should collect software.

The proposition that an academic library needs to deliberately create a coherent collection of computer-accessed information is ambitious. It is, however, rational and perhaps unavoidable. Given the growing importance of microcomputing in universities, someone on campus eventually will collect software, and this agency should have experience in assembling information for public use. The library is often the only organization able to take a sufficiently broad view of the university's information needs to make impartial collection decisions.

In creating a software collection the library reasserts its proper *role* as the organization in the university responsible for providing access to public knowledge, rather than its *stereotype* as the keeper of the books. An academic library can also earn a great deal of credibility with university administration and staff members in academic computing by undertaking the creation of a software collection.

A library that decides to assemble a collection of software and computer-accessed material, nevertheless, needs to acknowledge the difficulty of the task it is undertaking. Software is a complex and sometimes confusing format, carrying with it complications such as hardware compatibility, compatibility at the operating system level, and copyright and licensing restrictions. Creating a software collection is expensive. It confronts the library with many questions and consumes staff resources.

The answers to these questions are best obtained by specialists and, just as our library created an Information Technology Section to support the Microcomputer Center and assist with the overall automation of the library, it has encouraged the development of a software collection by establishing a new librarian position in the Public Services Department.

In the fall of 1984, a Computerized Data Files Librarian was hired with specific responsibilities for the creation and maintenance of the collection of computer-accessed materials. This position carries responsibilities distinct from those of normal collection development, which is divided by subject, because of the additional technical awareness required to handle computer formats, and because of the differences between software and print publishing and distribution channels. These differences and their implications are taken up in further detail in Chapter 4.

The charge to the new librarian was to keep abreast of the new technology, to analyze the varieties of computer-accessed information, to integrate this knowledge into the mission and collection philosophies of the library, and based upon that work to create a collection development policy for software and data files.

This chapter will treat the library's collection development policies for our permanent collection of software, shaped, as they are, by the library's priorities, our focus on information management, and the support of the research process. As is true of the library's general collections, the Microcomputer Center supports both a permanent collection of microcomputer software and data files on diskette and also a reserve collection. Most of the software packages in the reserve collection, which will be described in greater depth in Chapter 7, derive from faculty placements and thus closely reflect the needs of college courses. Through the presence of the reserve software collection in the Microcomputer Center, the library actually supports computer-based instruction in the colleges more broadly than the description of our collection development policies which follows might suggest.

Though it is perhaps presumptuous to codify policies in a field that changes so rapidly, the alternative is worse. We anticipated that a failure to plan for the collection of computer-accessed formats of information would result in institutional paralysis and no collection at all, or in a piecemeal approach to the collection of software that would be wasteful and inefficient. The challenge is to design a flexible collection development statement. If a library builds policy details on a solid base in the philosophies that govern its operations, changes can be made without altering the overall structure of the statement.

We describe our present collection development policy here with some hesitation. Our policy continues to evolve as we learn more and gain experience in the control of software. Nevertheless, we feel that our analysis, and the philosophies we used to create our collection development statement, are transferable and could serve as a guide or model for other institutions.

THE DEVELOPMENT OF A COLLECTION POLICY

In retrospect, the process we undertook to define a collection policy for software, computerized data files, and online resources was a taxonomic exercise of a somewhat schizophrenic sort. We analyzed the field of computer software and Mann's functions as a library, alternating between the "splitter" and the "lumper" schools of systematics. When describing an order or genus, "splitters" tend to subdivide their organisms into species and subspecies based on whatever minute differences they can identify. "Lumpers," on the other hand, try to group organisms together, taking the minute differences as individual variations. After extended deliberations as "splitters," we created a hierarchy of software. We then became "lumpers" and attempted to find parallels or similarities to the print materials in our collection. This allowed us to establish, whenever feasible, policies based on the precedents we had set with print materials.

Despite this approach, we quickly discovered that often there are no print equivalents for information appearing in machine-readable form. Even where print equivalents exist, the microcomputer may add an analytical capability, or intelligence, to the information it delivers. At present, that intelligence tends to be primitive and primarily calculative. But with future developments, including the application of artificial intelligence research to software, there will appear dimensions to the manipulation of research data that remain difficult to predict.

When we could not reasonably "lump" a genre of software with any print precedent, we went back to our basic premises and established policies for the new category.

This taxonomic metaphor can be extended to describe our continuing activity in collection development. As new "organisms" of microcomputer software emerge, we will integrate them into our systematics, "lumping" them into a previously described category when we can, or "splitting" them out and creating new policies when we must.

Our analysis was accomplished in a series of meetings of key staff members. To begin the taxonomic exercise we went back to our own origins, reviewing the library's primary mandate: "to provide information for the teaching and research needs of the university." Through trial and error, and many years of deliberation, we know to some degree what this means for the variety of print materials published. But when the same mission statement is applied to computer-accessed material, the implications are less obvious.

Next we reviewed genres of software as they appear in conventional sources. We considered how each category might support the library's mission. When possible, as noted above, we related software categories to print parallels. We found that we were not entirely satisfied with the existing schemes of categorizing microcomputer software and worked up one of our own. Gradually, after repeated discussion, we came to what we feel is a "Version 1.0" of our library world view of software.

The most common schemes of categorizing microcomputer software derive obviously from the applications of microcomputers in businesses and offices. Thus, we have word processors, spreadsheets, database managers, communications software, "integrated" packages, and so on. *The Whole Earth Software Catalog* took something of a stab at changing these pigeonholes with terms like "writing," "analyzing," and "organizing," but this scheme, although it may eliminate the jargon, does not offer a new perspective on what software is about. We felt that in order to encourage rational software selection decisions we would have to step back and create original divisions based on a broad, library-centered view of software.

THE CREATION OF THE TAXONOMY

We created our categories of software based on our focus on information, the *raison d'etre* of the library. Our first category was therefore raw information--machine-readable numerical and textual data. We subdivided this category according to whether the information is stored remotely, as it is with commercial online systems, or locally, and then further subdivided the local information by physical format. Our library, for instance, can store data on microcomputer diskette in the Microcomputer Center and also provide access to data sets on magnetic tape by having Cornell Computer Services archive the tapes and mount them as necessary on the university mainframes. We are beginning also to hold files residing on optical-disk or compact-disk media in the library.

Next, we tackled applications software for microcomputers. We defined general applications software as tools for clerical, calculative, and communications productivity. In many cases, these software packages now directly support the research process. The challenge was to determine the relevance of these programs to our collection. Thousands of programs fall under the definition of applications software and they all appeal differently to different audiences. A programmer looking at word-processing packages is interested in how the programs were written (their internal codes) and how software authors have employed different algorithms to solve the same problem. The business or office needing an accounting or spreadsheet program, in contrast, wants the one package that most closely matches its requirements.

The library, as an audience for software, falls somewhere between these two perspectives. First, although the library does conduct software evaluations, we do not feel that we are in a position to dictate which packages best meet the needs of our patrons. This leads us to purchase a variety of packages in many areas to support comparison and experimentation. Our interest in packages, however, focuses on what they do, rather than how they are programmed. Another important consideration for us is that our software library is intended to meet the needs of library patrons, and in particular their information needs, rather than to serve as a day-to-day working collection for internal library operations or as a support mechanism for college departments.

The key question is, of course, which types of programs to collect and how to weigh their respective merits in the selection process. Two primary factors currently drive our selection of software for the collection in the Microcomputer Center. The first is the needs of our student and faculty patrons. We feel obligated to provide access to the software packages that are most broadly used in the courses of our constituent colleges and divisions. We respond to student pressure for those productivity packages, such as word processors and spreadsheets, that help them complete papers and assignments. We must also provide sufficient numbers of the software packages that we teach to equip the Microcomputer Center's classroom for instruction.

In addition to these functions, we feel that the library's collection development decisions for microcomputer software must reflect and positively advance our primary mission of assisting people to access, retrieve, and control information. To this end, we have identified a spectrum of categories of applications programs, working from the premise introduced above--that programs perform different functions with regard to the "information" that is the basic concern of the library. From this perspective, we cannot consider applications programs themselves to constitute "information," in that researchers use the programs as tools to access or manipulate the information that is the true object of their work. The only exception would be a scholar engaged in the study of the structure of applications software, and this is not a large group among our clientele.

When we consider the acquisition of software related to the information-transfer function of the library, we are not responding to patron demand so much as we are trying to predict and even influence the development of information-related activities throughout the university community.

Our consideration of the relationship between microcomputer software and information led us to establish the following software categories: programs that record information according to the user's input (for instance, data-entry programs), programs that provide access to information (examples include communications and gateway software), programs that control information (bibliographic file managers), programs that analyze information (statistical packages), those that use information to solve problems (expert systems), those that transfer information or knowledge to people (as in Computer Assisted Instruction, or CAI, software), and the balance of programs that are unrelated to information transfer and control, including programs that generate or interpret programs.

For each of the above categories we defined the characteristics of the category, identified example programs, and decided on a collection policy. Where appropriate, we also assigned a collection level based upon a system of collection levels for software and machine-readable data structured to resemble the RLIN levels used with print materials. A 0 indicates no collection activity; 1, reference level works only; 2, general review works; 3, collections to support undergraduate and teaching activities; 4, research level collections, usually in selected languages; and 5, comprehensive collections, or all works published in the area in all languages.

For software, a reference level (1) would entail collecting one or two representative packages in a particular field; general and undergraduate/teaching levels (2 and 3) would lead us to purchase a selection of common packages; research level (4) means we collect a broader set of working and demonstration versions of programs; and comprehensive collection (5) indicates we expect to purchase all packages that we feel belong to a category, in either working or demonstration versions.

The remainder of this chapter is a category by category enumeration of our policies and collection levels.

CATAGORIES OF MACHINE-READABLE MATERIAL

Data

Data Stored Locally

Data are raw, unmanipulated numbers or text. They range from directory or reference information, to tables of numbers, to the full text of a journal or document. *The County and City Data Book* from the Census Bureau is available on floppy diskettes, as are the *Food and Nutrition Tables*. One can subscribe to product information on the computer industry that is supplied on diskette. Bibliographic and full-text files now also appear on compact disk, which will become an increasingly popular storage medium for published information.

These data have clear parallels to print material, making a collection policy easy to define. The library will collect materials falling within our subject scope, dependent upon the availability of acquisitions funds. We will duplicate print sources if the machine-readable format provides additional flexibility in data manipulation or analysis. Eventually we will also own data available only in machine-readable form.

Some data, especially the numeric sets, are accessed using database management or spreadsheet programs. Several standard "delimiters"--symbols or spaces--separate the individual data items in a file so that they can be read by common software. One of the factors affecting our decisions on the acquisition of applications packages will be which prove most useful, or become standard choices, in the manipulation of data sets. dBase III, Lotus 1-2-3, and Minitab are obvious examples of such programs at this time.

Online Data

Our library also "collects" remote data. Online text and numeric data, in addition to the more familiar bibliographic files, are increasingly valuable information resources to academics. As more data are stored in machine-readable files and as the software to search and retrieve information improves, it grows ever more imperative that libraries offer access to this information through computers and telecommunications links.

The full text of the *Journal of the Society of Architecture Historians* since 1941 is available online. Users can query numeric/time series such as the Chase Econometrics Energy Database or the U.S. census statistics on Donnelley. There are currently thousands of online reference and numeric databases, such as the Coalink database, which contains financial, transportation, and production information on coal. More databases appear every month.

Online systems raise service and collection issues for the library. In providing information services to patrons who work in disciplines supported by online databases, a library must consider whether it is obligated to provide access to these systems. Often online files are only available in machine-readable form, with no print alternatives. Failure to provide access to such information resources can thus leave a patron with no alternative.

Two different pricing schemes are in general use in the world of online information: pay-as-used and subscription. Under both schemes the initial investment required of the library consists of the start-up costs of purchasing manuals and securing passwords, and the personnel costs involved in training staff to use the system. Subsequently the costs of the pay-as-used online system run in direct proportion to the use of the system. The subscription database costs a set fee whether or not the system is actually used and regardless of the level of use. The charge thus resembles a minimum-use charge more than it does a serial subscription.

Both schemes raise the perennial question of who pays for the service. This is not an appropriate forum for an in-depth discussion, but the major issues merit mention. Does the patron pay for the full cost of a search (i.e., search time, staff time, and overhead) or just the direct costs? If the library pays for part of the costs, what will the source of funds be? Should the money come from the regular acquisitions budget or a separate budget for online services? At Mann Library we have decided, for the present, to absorb staff costs in the overall library budget, to pay for the indirect costs of database searching out of our software acquisitions budget, and to charge direct costs to the patron.

We are currently "collecting" online databases as we do local data, if the subject falls within our scope. By collecting we mean obtaining access to the database. The consideration of whether a particular database is worth the investment in staff time to learn the new system influences our decision. The library evaluates subscription databases periodically to see if they are generating enough use to make the subscription worthwhile.

Applications Programs

Information-Related Programs

PROGRAMS THAT RECORD INFORMATION. Programs that convert data to machine-readable form can be described, for our purposes, as information recorders. Examples of such programs are data-entry packages, which provide templates or blank forms for consistent record input, and word processors, which allow the user to enter and manipulate text, including anything from letters and memos to articles and books. Another variation is the data collection program. These packages function as electronic laboratory notebooks and are sometimes capable of accepting readings under program control from scientific instruments attached to the computer.

Programs in this category are marginal to the collection scope we have defined for the library. We collect those packages that serve as adjuncts to programs we do consider critical to our role as an organization that provides people access to, and trains them to control, information. An example would be word-processing programs that can generate or reformat bibliographic records for subsequent loading into a bibliographic file manager.

We also feel an obligation to secure those programs in this area that are in common use at Cornell, for the convenience of our patrons. The Microcomputer Center's collection thus includes the word-processing packages that students typically use in the preparation of papers, though we do not feel that this is central to our *library* function.

PROGRAMS THAT PROVIDE ACCESS TO INFORMATION. Access to machine-readable information occurs on two levels, remote and local. At present there are two principal types of programs that provide access to remote databases: general communications packages and destination-specific gateway programs.

Communications programs establish protocols for data transfer between computers. Protocols determine the amount of information to be sent in each transmission cycle, the convention for error checking, whether transmitted characters are displayed on screen at either end of the transmission, and the specific data-formatting requirements of the machines involved in the data exchange. The crudest communications packages turn a microcomputer into a "dumb terminal" connected to a mainframe host. Most communications packages go beyond this and automate some of the process of online communications. They may dial the host computer or execute a "macro" sequence to log into an online system. Most programs are able to save the information from an online session onto a diskette in a process known as downloading.

Some communications programs have been tailored to facilitate access to specific online systems. These programs, called "gateway systems" or "search aids," can be viewed as a synthesis of the information in the printed search manuals distributed by the vendors of online systems and the communication program needed to access those systems. Gateway programs function one layer deeper into the search process than do generic communications programs. As search aids, these programs can translate local commands into the search languages of several vendor systems, thus permitting the user to work with one set of "universal" commands. Gateway packages facilitate the downloading of search results, and often allow one to structure searches offline, under the control of the software running on the microcomputer. These canned searches can then be saved and passed to the online system at the user's convenience.

For both communications programs and gateways or search aids, we are collecting selected packages pertinent to our online search activities, whether they are conducted by librarians or end-users. The more sophisticated gateway systems are of particular interest in that they may serve as a partial substitute for the librarian's function as an intermediary to online databases, and as a supplement to our instructional programs in online searching.

Indexing programs for microcomputers provide access to information that is stored locally. Vendors sometimes bundle these programs with word processors, but they may also be purchased separately and so constitute a distinct category of software. Indexing programs generate a list of terms cross referenced to pages in a document. We collect representative samples of these programs in demonstration or working versions. An emerging genre of software in this category is search-and-retrieval systems designed to work with data files on compact disk. It appears that in most cases vendors will provide a particular search package with the data sets they offer. The library will thus necessarily acquire software of this type as we begin to secure information stored on compact and optical disk.

PROGRAMS THAT CONTROL INFORMATION. In general, the programs that we place in this category are what the software industry calls "database managers." An important subgroup for us would be bibliographic file managers. Database management programs, designed to control both textual and numeric data, typically work most effectively with information that can be segmented into discrete fields for manipulation. Programs vary in capability. Some are the computerized equivalent of a card file. At their most powerful, database managers provide sophisticated text manipulation, the ability to perform complex numeric calculations, Boolean search functions, flexible report generation, and a structured command language. Substantial programming skills are usually required to exploit the full potential of these programs.

Database management programs are of interest in the library information environment for two reasons: as mentioned above, data on diskette are sometimes formatted to be "read" by the popular database management programs, and, more fundamentally, these programs exist to organize information. For both reasons we are collecting selected working packages.

Bibliographic file managers are database managers that specifically address the control of literature citations. They typically provide a text-editing environment as well as search-and-retrieval capabilities. These programs support variable length fields. Record control is optimized for textual, rather than numeric, manipulations. To summarize the full definition of these programs we will present in Chapter 11: bibliographic file managers are able to import external data files (such as those downloaded from online searches), accept data input from the keyboard, search the citations in a database, and generate reports in citation style formats rather than tables.

Since these programs perform traditional library functions on a microcomputer, they are of high interest to us. Bibliographic file managers are also of considerable interest to faculty. We are attempting to assemble a comprehensive collection of working and demonstration versions of programs that perform all of the functions listed above, and also to collect selected working and demonstration versions of programs that support some of the desired functions. The library offers workshops in the use of bibliographic file managers for the control of reprint collections and provides consulting support in this software genre to Cornell faculty members and students. Details appear in Chapter 11.

PROGRAMS THAT ANALYZE INFORMATION. Programs in this category are divided into two sections: general and subject-specific.

Most general information analysis programs are numerical in orientation. Examples include spreadsheets and statistical analysis packages. We experience great demand from patrons for access to these programs, which they use to analyze their own data in connection with course work or research projects. Here, as with the category of programs that record information, our selection decisions are currently driven primarily by what students and faculty members request. In addition, information analysis packages are useful as tools for interpreting raw data, so we are purchasing selected "standard" packages for use with data sets.

The second area of information analysis, subject-specific programs, is a huge field. These programs fall on a continuum between what we may term "analysis software" and "decision aids." The position of a particular program on the scale depends on the proportion of user input to machine intelligence.

At one end of the spectrum are analysis packages consisting of resident formulae to which the user passes data for the program to process. The program is no more than a book of formulae and a robot calculator.

At the other end of the scale are the decision aids--programs with both resident data and formulae, to which the user may add more data. A program performs calculations based on the input data using its resident formulae and data, and in a manner of speaking "interprets" the results. Diet analysis programs are an excellent example of decision-aid programs. They contain food content tables from the U.S. Department of Agriculture, data on minimum daily requirements for various age and sex groups, and algorithms to analyze diets as indicated by the user. The user inputs food eaten and the program examines the diet for things like missing nutrients and calorie intake.

Within our collection scope, we purchase representative examples of analysis and decision-aid programs. We try to avoid collecting many programs that employ similar analysis formulae. Decision-aid packages show greater variety because differences in the resident data add a level of complexity to the programs. Thus, if there are interesting variations in the combination of data and formulae in decision-aid software, we are willing to acquire several programs in one subject area.

PROGRAMS THAT USE INFORMATION TO SOLVE PROBLEMS. Expert systems, usually composed of two elements--an "inference engine" and a knowledge base--are the one genre of software we currently place in this information category, but expert systems for microcomputers are growing rapidly in importance. With an expert system, users translate their expertise into a form the computer can apply to problems by establishing a set of "if/then" logical relationships (the inference engine) and a body of pertinent information (the knowledge base). Using the "rules" of the inference engine, other users can extract information from the knowledge base. These programs are an excellent example of how the "intelligence" of a machine can enhance the information it stores.

Expert systems provide "value added" information retrieval service. At a primitive level, they can perform some of the tasks of reference librarians or expert consultants, and as such they are of interest in the field of information retrieval. Because of this potential, the library is seeking to include a broad spectrum of these packages in its software collection.

PROGRAMS THAT TRANSFER INFORMATION TO PEOPLE. In essence, educational programs, or computer aided instruction (CAI) packages, automate the learning process. CAI packages require no additional data from the user. The programs judge the correctness of the user's answers and issue appropriate responses. Just as we do not purchase printed programmed learning texts, we do not purchase in this area except in exceptional cases, and then only to support the activities of specific courses in our constituent colleges. Faculty are free to place CAI packages in our reserve software collection for course use.

Programs That Generate or Interpret Programs

Most packages used by systems analysts and programmers do not fall within our collection scope, as we define it in terms of the library's information-related activities. Programs in this category include assemblers, compilers, programming development aids, program generators, programmers' utilities, and authoring programs. These packages help programmers do their work, but are not directly useful in the control of information. We collect in this area to meet the needs of students doing course work in our client colleges.

We also collect some operating systems and utility programs, where these serve as working programs for the operation of the Microcomputer Center or assist patrons in such activities as the retrieval of lost files.

Productivity Applications in Business and Engineering

The library does not consider programs produced for business and engineering productivity to be of direct application to the types of information retrieval and control that we see as central to our mission. For example, we are not collecting financial, accounting, inventory, administrative, or personnel administration packages. CAD/CAM and graphics are also outside our collection scope. We only consider purchases in these areas when a software package is necessary for the support of a college course, and in most cases we would expect the sponsoring academic department to provide the package for software reserve.

In summary, the library's collection development policy for microcomputer software and online information resources attempts to meet several distinct needs. We obviously have to provide a software environment that will support our instructional activities. Further, we try to meet the demands of the faculty and students for productivity software, insofar as our acquisition budget will allow. Beyond this, we are committed to creating a collection of software that reflects the library's concern with the provision of access to information, its retrieval, and its control. This final concern led us to create a tentative set of categories of software based not on existing divisions, but on the relationship of software to information.

We fully expect to reexamine the relative weight that we accord to acquisitions activity in our various categories of microcomputer software, based on changes in the nature and quality of the packages that become available in the marketplace. It is also possible that we will feel compelled to revise our software "taxonomy," or to add new software categories. Nevertheless, we feel that if a library is to shape a collection of software that has some philosophical integrity, it must determine the spectrum of software it will seek to provide and the relationship between the software collection and the information resources that are the traditional concern of the library.

SUMMARY

1. Increasingly, microcomputer software is tied closely to the provision and control of information. In many cases, software contains information of interest to academic researchers. Academic libraries should therefore collect software as a natural extension of their traditional mandate to collect, preserve, organize, and provide access to information.

2. External databases are also becoming an information resource of great importance to researchers. The question of how to pay for providing information from online sources is one that each library must answer within its institutional environment, but external databases now fall within the purview of collection development policy.

3. The development and support of a software collection requires time, money, and technical expertise. In most cases this will mean new staff or substantial training for existing staff. Our library created an Information Technology Section and the position of Computerized Data Files Librarian to help contend with these needs.

4. The collection of software and online information resources should be systematic. The volatility and complexity of these marketplaces should not lead a library away from its basic collection development principles. A library should consider the spectrum of software packages and information resources available in the marketplace, create meaningful categories for collection development activity, and assign collection levels to these categories.

5. Several approaches to the categorization of software currently exist, and others are possible. Most present schemes emerge from the focus of the current software marketplace on the needs of business. Our library, feeling that existing software categories would not suit our collection development requirements, developed categories based on the relationship between software and the information that is the *raison d'etre* of the library. Our categories provide for both machine-readable data files and computer programs. They also accommodate both microcomputer-based software and external online resources.

6. In deciding how to treat the collection of materials in the various categories it creates, a library does well to consider its basic philosophies for the provision of access to information and precedents set with print materials. It is also well to be aware, however, that computerized control of information may make possible manipulations that far exceed what can be accomplished with so-called print equivalents.

Chapter 4

The Selection and Acquisition of Software and Computerized Data

Katherine Chiang and Howard Curtis

SOFTWARE SELECTION

In the initial stages of developing our software collection, the library has, as suggested in Chapter 3, concentrated on a core collection of "generic" applications packages. As our collection grows and the computerized information needs of our research faculties become clearer, more of what we acquire will be subject-specific software in a variety of disciplines. In addition, a greater proportion of what we purchase will consist of data files rather than software packages as such.

Though the library's overall collection development model assigns responsibility by subject rather than format, we have assigned computer-readable formats to just two selectors (the Computerized Data Files Librarian and the Computer Projects Coordinator). The library believes the decision to treat collecting responsibilities for computer-readable materials separately was a proper response in the first phase of software collection development, given the background and technical skills required to perform the job, as outlined in Chapter 3. In contrast to reviews of print material, most of the current awareness literature (advertisements, reviews, etc.) for software and computerized data files still appears in computer magazines. The creation of a coherent set of collection development and service policies for software is best handled by one or two people. It is difficult, moreover, to function as a software selector until one has worked extensively with a microcomputer, and when the Microcomputer Center opened, few of our Public Service librarians had this experience.

These conditions will change with time. In the future, a librarian's computer skills will likely include more than familiarity with the bibliographic utilities or online systems. Librarians will develop an understanding of microcomputers and software packages. Trends in software, data publishing, advertising, and evaluation will clarify themselves, allowing libraries to select computer-readable materials in the same manner as they do the balance of the collection. Once a library has established a groundwork of policies and most selectors are comfortable with software, collection development responsibilities can be distributed to the subject selectors, who will then make subsequent decisions concerning selection priorities through the usual mechanisms. We hope to complete this transition within two to three years at our library.

What follows in the remainder of the first half of this chapter is a treatment of the issues and general trends in selection. This will be more valuable than a description of our current collection procedures, which are specific to our library and will go quickly out of date.

Issues in Selection

If the software that a library purchases is to constitute a functional collection, it must run on computers readily available to the patron. This need for hardware support, together with the peculiar characteristics of software publication, raises several issues. For example, will the library purchase packages that do not run on its hardware and, potentially, make these available for out-of-the-building loan?

Our library decided to acquire only software packages that run on our computers--currently IBM PCs, Apple Macintoshes, and DEC Rainbows. Although, as noted in Chapter 1, several of our machines also contain boards that support Apple II and CP/M software, we try to avoid these packages wherever we have an alternative, in the interest of user convenience.

Microcomputer software thus presents libraries with a unique problem in that software requires the presence of a particular computer running a particular operating system. When the operating system or the machine becomes obsolete, a library will find itself facing a difficult choice--support an antiquated operating environment or render a portion of the collection inoperable. No other library format suffers the same threat of mass extinction.

Another issue arises from the frequency with which software publishers release editions. Each improvement or "fix" to the program is potentially a new version. A selector must determine whether changes are important enough that the library should buy the new version, and whether the producer will support previous versions. For some heavily used packages, selection requires a financial commitment similar to that for serials or textbooks. Not only do "upgrades" cost money, but the library must also invest the staff time and materials necessary to configure them for use.

The appearance of new versions or upgrades to programs also presents libraries with an archival issue. Many software vendors offer a discount on the latest version of a program only to customers who return the program diskettes from the previous version. This policy prevents the use of the old software on a different machine, but it may cause problems for a library which takes its archival responsibilities seriously. Should the library bargain with the vendor to be permitted to keep the old program version in a special archival collection? Should the library simply purchase the new version at full price, retaining all its rights to the use of the old version but incurring substantially higher charges?

Selectors will also encounter problems coping with the short lifespan of some software publishers. In this regard, software houses resemble small presses. It is difficult to ascertain just what the producers are offering, how much their programs cost, and what the programs will do. When a software publisher folds, technical support for what may be a number of complex packages also disappears.

Sources for Selectors

The issues treated above are general in import; they stand prior to the problem of making the best choice among the software packages available. At the level of packages or data sets, the library encounters two primary categories of selection questions: (1) Is there a program that will do X? (2) If there is more than one program that can do X, which is best? To answer these questions we use two major sources: published information (both print and electronic) and expert advice. In addition, we must sometimes undertake software evaluation in the library to answer the second question.

Published Sources, Print and Electronic

Since our major acquisitions activity to date has been in the area of applications programs, our primary published sources have been the articles, reviews, and advertisements that appear in software and microcomputer journals. The most current information is found in the advertisements and "announcements" of new software packages, but, short of requesting a demonstration diskette, it is difficult to evaluate quality until reviews begin to emerge. When we are seeking an application program of a specific type, we also use software catalogs (print and online) to locate programs. These are useful for comparison and awareness as well. Both BRS and DIALOG have a software "file" (SOFT and MENU respectively). *The Software Catalog* by Elsevier and the *Datapro Directory of Microcomputer Software* are examples of general content print directories. Of course, we rarely order the version of the program listed in the catalog, in that it has generally been superceded since the catalog was published.

The quality and coverage of published sources for subject software varies. Catalogs dedicated to applications software with a business slant rarely list subject-specific software comprehensively, particularly in scientific fields. The articles and advertisements in subject journals--especially those that focus on computing in their field--are good sources. Electronic bulletin boards and private databases from scientific associations and institutes are a possible source, though it is difficult to gauge the reliability of the information they contain.

Experts

Personal contact is an essential method of gathering information in a rapidly moving field. By the time information appears in print it is often outdated. Many publishers of software reviews hold manuscripts for review and editing for three to six months after submission, creating a substantial time lag. If one adds to this the weeks or months required to learn a software package and perform an evaluation, a library that depends on print sources or selection information alone may find itself purchasing software as it begins to fade into obsolescence.

At many universities, the academic computing center evaluates software. Computing center personnel are usually aware of and provide consulting services in those programs heavily used on campus. Faculty members active in computing are oftentimes members of a departmental computing committee. We consider such committees a valuable source of information. At Cornell, college and interdisciplinary computing committees are also good places to contact knowledgeable people. As computing comes to play a broader role in course work, faculty interests not only reveal what software products play a part in the research process but also predict future student demands for software.

Another concentration of computing "activists" will be found in campus user groups, especially those dedicated to academic as opposed to office productivity concerns. A knowledge of who on campus is writing and using what software is crucial for the creation of a quality library collection.

Faculty members and students are usually more than willing to share their experiences with microcomputer programs and to make recommendations. From among the people one encounters at service desks, in classes and workshops, or through users groups, a selector can develop a network of useful contacts. Patrons, in addition to sharing experiences, often want to make software purchase requests at the library. We have thus prepared a Software Purchase Recommendation Form similar to that used for books but with added "technical" questions. Requests are evaluated against our collection development standards, and patrons notified of our decision and its rationale.

Commercial consultants for specific types of software are growing more numerous. An example from our subject area is the farm computer consultant who offers advice on hardware and software to farmers to help them meet their computing needs. Some consultants are actually distributors for particular hardware or software firms, and thus a dubious source because of their bias. Those consultants who evaluate software in order to recommend solutions to clients, however, are a potential source of information.

There are as well numerous national organizations that deal with software, data resources, and computing. Examples would include the Inter-university Consortium for Political and Social Research (ICPSR), located in Ann Arbor, the Northeast Computer Institute in Pennsylvania, and the Association of Agricultural Computing Companies. These organizations generally concentrate on a particular subject area. Depending on their mission and ambitions, they may function as clearinghouses, archives, or consortia. The information they issue ranges from occasional newsletters to online databases.

An expensive but effective method of keeping very current is to attend computing conferences. For comprehensive collections in a particular field, personal contact with the vendors producing the programs is the only sure means of keeping abreast of developments.

The Comparative Evaluation of Software

If the library needs a piece of print data available from just one source, the decision to buy involves only a consideration of whether the library can afford the item. The same situation pertains with an applications package that is functionally unique. If, however, several programs exist that perform the required function, a library may find that it needs to undertake comparative evaluation.

The evaluation of packages for addition to a library collection differs from the kind of evaluation that an office or library department looking for a specific application for in-house use would perform. General evaluation criteria for software have been outlined in the literature. A succinct summary of general criteria, for example, appears in an article by Jane Anne Hannigan.[1] Hannigan proposes the following criteria:

1. Does the program do what it says it will do?
2. Does it make use of the computer in an appropriate fashion?

3. Does the software require additional hardware in order to run satisfactorily?
4. Is the documentation clear and communicative?
   Will back-up services be available to the purchaser?
5. Is there a satisfactory reason to purchase the software for the institution?

An additional question in cases where data are included, either as the full content of the item (disk or online) or as the resident data of an applications program, is the validity and integrity of that data.

To supplement criteria at this level of abstraction, software selectors may wish to develop guidelines for the evaluation of certain genres or subject areas of software. Stating the general principles of software evaluation is reasonably straightforward. The difficulties appear when a selector wishes to compare programs that meet the basic requirements.

A substantial investment of time is required to familiarize oneself with a category of software, though such familiarity is essential to meaningful evaluation. If fortunate, the selector will find a recent comparative review of programs of the kind under consideration. If the article is good it will give a description of what a program should do and of how the reviewed programs measure up to that standard. The selector can then evaluate additional programs against the same standards to update the review. Lacking a good comparative review, individual program reviews can be used to compile a standard against which other programs may be evaluated.

All too often there are no reviews, or no current ones, and no contacts familiar with the category of programs under consideration. In this case the selector has to do the whole comparative review. From demonstration versions, or, ideally, full-fledged versions of pertinent programs, a set of review standards must be compiled. The selector has to learn how to use the software and create a set of standards based on that experience. This process is valuable in that it makes the selector thoroughly familiar with a portion of the library's software collection, but it takes an immense amount of time. The selector must carefully identify when such a labor-intensive, hands-on evaluation is justified. As more selectors become involved with software, library administrators may wish to create formal guidelines that fix when such evaluations are to be undertaken and how much time they may consume.

If the library does undertake detailed software evaluation, the results are often publishable. At a minimum, some kind of written account of the performance of the packages considered should be made available to the university community. At Mann Library, for instance, we have established criteria for the evaluation of bibliographic file managers. This topic is treated in further detail in Chapter 10.

SOFTWARE ACQUISITIONS

As stated in Chapter 3, the library does not discriminate against sources of information because of their format. The library seeks, wherever possible, to treat microcomputer software and data files on diskette as it does more traditional formats--books, journals, cassettes, video tapes, and so on. In the area of acquisitions, these assumptions led us to conclude that the library should order software and data files through the standard channel--the Acquisitions Department.

Microcomputer software remains a new format of information that presents a library with difficulties in the acquisitions process. In fact, we have not achieved our goal of integrating software into overall acquisitions activity as of this writing (December 1986) because of a number of practical obstacles--some of which derive from the policies of Cornell University, and some from procedures and regulations in the software industry. We will review both sets of concerns here, in that Cornell's approach to the purchase of microcomputer software is probably parallel to trends in other universities.

Information and University Purchasing Procedures

The microcomputer revolution--in the form of the dedicated word processor--hit departmental offices at Cornell before it began to change the face of academic computing. Dedicated word processors may have transformed document preparation forever, but they did not challenge existing university purchasing procedures. As the text-processing "software" was built in as an integral part of the machine, buying a word processor, from the standpoint of university purchasing rules, was no different from buying a typewriter. The word processor was an item of "equipment," pure and simple.

A department that wanted a word processor, or any other piece of equipment, would explore the market, make an initial decision as to its preference, and file a requisition for the purchase of a particular model from a particular vendor. A university accounting office then checked the requisition to confirm that the department had funds in its accounts sufficient to cover the purchase and passed the paperwork on to the university Purchasing Department. It was the responsibility of Purchasing to review the vendor and the price on the requisition and approve the department's request, or, if possible, to negotiate a better price with the same or a different vendor. In some cases, Purchasing would suggest an alternative product if appropriate. After the approval or modification of a requisition, Purchasing would issue a purchase order and send a copy to the vendor of choice.

With the introduction of general-purpose microcomputers, this model began to fall apart. The computer, the printer, and the other pieces of hardware in a typical computer system were obviously equipment, but software, which was equally essential, was not so easily defined. Software was simply information recorded on floppy diskettes. It had a transient and modifiable quality, making it difficult to place in the equipment category. In the early days, software purchased with computer hardware was classified as equipment, and thus subject to Purchasing review, while software purchased at some later date was treated as "materials and supplies." In addition to the obvious intellectual contradiction, this approach caused difficulties in the bookkeeping for sponsored grants and contracts, since supplies but not equipment qualify as "indirect costs." In late 1984, the university decided, because of the substantial cost of microcomputer software and its status as an "important asset to the university," that software would be treated as equipment whenever its price exceeded a certain minimum. This served to tighten record-keeping requirements for software and made major software orders uniformly subject to review by the Purchasing Department.

Given the expense of software, its importance to a functioning microcomputer system, and the complexity of the licensing terms that surround its use, this was undoubtedly a healthy decision. The new ruling presented a problem, however, to any university library that sought to acquire software as a component of its collection, since library acquisitions have traditionally stood outside review by the Purchasing Department to facilitate the ordering of materials and to guarantee that the libraries are free to secure whatever information they deem essential to the mission of the university.

The library viewed this as a serious issue. Also, since we would be the first unit of the campus libraries to purchase software for patron access rather than staff use, we would be setting an important precedent. We informed Cornell Purchasing when we began to buy software packages for the Microcomputer Center's collection in the spring of 1984 that we considered the purchase of this software to be a component of library acquisitions activity. Thus, while we might consult with Purchasing from time to time on sources and advantageous pricing arrangements, our orders would not ultimately be subject to Purchasing review. Cornell Purchasing accepted this position, leaving the library free to secure software as a true component of its information resources.

Though this resolution removed the major institutional obstacle to our treating software purchases as part of our overall acquisitions activity, it did not eliminate the many difficulties of dealing with the representatives of the microcomputer software industry. First, because the public-access environment of the Microcomputer Center makes it impossible for us to respect all the terms of standard software licensing agreements, we feel obligated to inform vendors in detail of the procedures we use to control software loans in the center. This involves attaching two sheets of explanatory text to each order for a software package. This documentation appears in the Appendix.

Many software houses offer educational or instructional discounts on their products. The terms of these discounts are various and sometimes involve individual negotiation. Because these negotiations often require technical knowledge and a detailed understanding of the operation of the Microcomputer Center, they are the responsibility of the Microcomputer Center Manager at this time. While it is of course possible to cultivate the necessary expertise in an acquisitions department, the negotiations can consume a good deal of time and differ from traditional acquisitions activities. It is likely at our library that even after the Acquisitions Department has begun to order software, the staff of the Information Technology Section, and, in some cases, Public Services, will conduct negotiations with software vendors when these prove necessary.

The terms of payment on software orders have caused the library a second set of problems. Although the software house that expects payment in cash in a California garage appears to be losing market share to the big players, many vendors still demand payment in advance. Software discount houses are growing accustomed to institutional customers, but still prefer to deal with those prepared to charge purchases against a credit card. These arrangements present difficulties for business organizations, or universities, that issue purchase orders to initiate transactions and pay against an invoice produced by the vendor.

These problems in processing software orders have caused the library to retain the generation and handling of the orders in the Administrative Office, which routinely processes orders for equipment and supplies, even though the university has given us permission, in effect, to proceed with software orders as a component of library acquisitions. In the next year, we expect to move to a more standard acquisitions model. With the major software suppliers beginning to improve their mechanisms for handling major corporate and institutional accounts, the acquisition of software will more closely resemble the standard publications model. This evolution in the industry, we hope, will help us to effect a smooth transition in our acquisitions work, from Administrative Office to Acquisitions Department.

SUMMARY

1. Even if a library normally divides selection responsibilities by subject area, it may wish to assign the *format* of software to one or two people on a temporary basis. As librarians become more familiar with microcomputers and software, a restoration of the subject-based model for software becomes possible, and probably desirable.

2. Microcomputer software and data files raise a number of selection issues. For instance:

> Software requires hardware support. How will the library provide patrons with access to hardware?

> Will the library support obsolescent hardware and operating system environments in order to avoid consigning a portion of its software collection to oblivion?

> How will the library treat multiple editions of a program? How will it deal with the failure of software publishers?

3. Selection sources for microcomputer software include print and online resources and human experts. A library should seek advice from faculty members involved in academic computing, campus computing groups, university consortia, and possibly commercial consultants. Conferences are an excellent source of current information.

4. A library may occasionally wish to undertake comparative evaluation of software packages. This activity can yield distinct benefits in professional expertise and publications, but is time consuming. The library should set clear guidelines that indicate when it will undertake software evaluation and how the results of the work will be made available to its clientele.

5. Though universities may lump software purchases with those of equipment or supplies, if a library truly considers software to be part of the collection, it must treat software as an information resource. This may mean seeking partial or full exemption from the restrictions and review procedures that govern software purchases by other university organizations.

6. A library should move to integrate software purchases into its overall acquisitions activity, though institutional constraints and the state of the software industry may force compromise for the near-term future.

Note

1. Jane Anne Hannigan, "Evaluation of Microcomputer Software," *Library Trends* 33: 335-36 (Winter 1985).

Chapter 5

Copyright and Legal Considerations

Samuel Demas

THE PHILOSOPHICAL CONTEXT

Democracy is based on the participation of an informed citizenry in the governmental process, and this requires open access to information. The principle of freedom of access to information, regardless of one's ability to pay, finds its most concrete expression in our system of public libraries and in the cooperation among libraries of all types.

In making information freely available through libraries, society must protect the property rights of authors and publishers to assure an adequate financial incentive to the producers and purveyors of published knowledge. This is accomplished through copyright law. Unlike European copyright law, which centers around protecting the rights of authors, U.S. copyright legislation stems from the constitutional mandate to promote science and the arts. The concept of "fair use" of copyrighted material essentially provides an entitlement of citizens to free access to information.[1]

One can argue that the control of machine-readable information, including the copying of microcomputer software and the downloading of information from online databases, is simply a variant of the classic copyright issues. In addressing the special problems of photocopy machines and videocassette recorders, the copyright law has already responded to intellectual property issues which, though they involve technical differences, are conceptually parallel to those surrounding print materials. Nevertheless, the copyright law as currently written is inadequate to the task of regulating control and access to machine-readable formats.

In order to protect their enormous investments and assure profits, producers of software and online databases are turning to bodies of law other than copyright: contract, patent, and trade secret law. In so doing, they are taking the question of access to information out of the realm of public policy and entitlement and framing patterns of access based purely on business interests and principles that derive from commerce in commodities. For example, some software publishers affix licenses to their shrink-wrap packaging which restrict use of a program diskette to one machine. Certain copy-protection schemes prevent the creation of an archival copy of the program the customer has purchased. Database producers routinely promulgate contract clauses which prohibit any form of downloading from their databases without their specific written consent.

None of these restrictions has any basis in copyright law; they stem from the contract law specified in license agreements. If libraries agree to the terms of such licenses and contracts, they should be prepared to live with the restrictions stipulated within them. The danger is that libraries will acquiesce to restrictions which undermine the freedom of access to information on which our society is based. Establishing equitable policies for use of software is just the first round in what will be a long, complex struggle to determine how electronic information is regulated in our society. As Jennifer Slack has argued, "In the establishment of institutional structures to accommodate the transfer and control of computer hardware and software, patterns of power, control, dependency, and domination are being forged."[2]

If the present trend continues, there is a risk that a class of "information poor" citizens will emerge. Many people may not be able to pay the high cost of computerized information. Libraries may find themselves unable to afford to subsidize access to all types of information, and may also be constrained by business law in performing their mission of freely providing citizens with access to information. Just as libraries have worked to protect the public's right to uncensored information, they must serve as advocates for equitable access to computer-based information resources. Librarians have a unique and pivotal role to play in intellectual property matters. In the case of software, we are the only organized, institutionalized voice speaking for the rights of end-users.

New information technologies are developing faster than the laws that regulate their use. For example, the copyright law does not specifically address many of the questions surrounding microcomputer software and online databases. Establishing a microcomputer center immediately throws a library into the struggle to define the laws and practices regulating the use and ownership of information in machine-readable formats.

The transition to new information formats and technologies thus presents a challenge and an opportunity for academic libraries. This chapter will focus on problems of intellectual property rights for computer-based information of direct concern to libraries that create microcomputer centers: (1) the evolving commercial software market, (2) legal protections for microcomputer software, (3) policy and procedural considerations for a collection of microcomputer software, and (4) copyright and online databases. What follows is an overview of copyright and licensing considerations for software libraries and end-user database searching programs, with guidelines for policy formulation.

While the pertinent laws and issues are briefly outlined, nothing in this chapter should be taken as legal advice. The opinions and conclusions contained in this chapter are those of the author and do not necessarily represent the views and conclusions of Mann Library or Cornell University. The author is not a lawyer and the contents of this publication should not be construed as legal advice, which libraries are encouraged to obtain from their own counsel. Points of law are elaborated only to provide a context for the formulation of library policy during this transitional period in the history of publishing and copyright. The chapter concludes with a discussion of several issues and trends which the reader will wish to follow in this evolving field.

THE SOFTWARE INDUSTRY, THE MARKETPLACE, AND LIBRARIES

The microcomputer software industry is still young. It changes rapidly. Industry standards and realistic pricing structures are gradually evolving but a mature new branch of the publishing industry has yet to emerge. The financial stakes in software are high, as the primary source of revenue for the computer industry is shifting from hardware to software. The software market is estimated at four billion dollars per year. The demand for microcomputer software is growing and thousands of entrepreneurs are jockeying for their share of the market.

While software publication and sales would logically seem to belong to the publishing industry, the computer industry currently publishes most microcomputer software. Unlike established publishers, software houses have little experience with trade in intellectual property and try to apply the laws and strategies of the consumer marketplace to scholarly information.

There are many signs that the software industry remains immature. Software vendors attempt to control every aspect of the market and to strictly control the use and duplication of their products. There are virtually no consumer protection laws specifically governing software. The warranties offered by many software vendors say, in effect, that the company guarantees nothing and disclaims any responsibility for the product beyond the replacement of physically flawed diskettes. Much software is generally acknowledged to be overpriced, in part to compensate for exaggerated claims of the impact of software piracy on the market. To prevent piracy the industry is experimenting with extremely restrictive and practically unenforceable license agreements and a variety of hardware- and software-based copy protection schemes. Through their trade association, the Association of Data Processing Service Organizations (ADAPSO), software vendors are selecting cases of copy infringement and bringing suit to frighten users into strict adherence to license agreements.

The future, however, will bring moderating influences. High prices and unrealistic license terms are producing a consumer backlash that is already forcing the software industry to adopt a more reasonable approach. It appears that the software market is evolving; users are exerting more influence and software producers are losing their ability to control the marketplace. The demand for more flexible, realistic site licenses is growing intense in the corporate community. Consumer protection legislation is being proposed, while the software industry itself is showing signs of making accommodations to the realities of the market.

One market which software publishers have largely ignored is that of the library or academic microcomputer center. The lack of thought about this small but significant outlet for their products is evident in the restrictions imposed by standard software licenses. It is the responsibility of librarians to educate the software industry about the purpose and value of software libraries and microcomputer centers. Once vendors understand that library borrowing is not simply a substitute for the purchase of software but can actually provide visibility to an excellent new product, they listen.

To gain a hearing from the software industry, libraries must demonstrate their sensitivity to the rights of software authors and publishers and must have a clear understanding of the laws and issues that surround intellectual property rights and machine-readable information formats.

FORMS OF LEGAL PROTECTION FOR MICROCOMPUTER SOFTWARE

Software differs from other types of library materials in that copyright is not the only or necessarily the most effective means software authors and publishers use to protect their rights of ownership. As suggested above, four different bodies of law are potentially applicable: patent, trade secret, contract, and copyright. Copyright and contract law are the most commonly used methods of protection for microcomputer software.

Copyright

Copyright is federal protection of intellectual property. The Copyright Revision Act of 1976 is the body of federal copyright legislation and contains special provisions for library copying rights and for the copying of library materials by the public. However, the act does not specifically address computer programs and was subsequently amended with the passage of Section 117, the Computer Software Copyright Act of 1980.

Several sections of the Copyright Revision Act of 1976, including 107 and 108, are pertinent to the use of microcomputer software in a library. Educational institutions rely heavily on the "fair use" exemption in Section 107 to make multiple copies of printed materials for classroom use and to justify limited copying for reserve reading operations. The guidelines that determine fair use include "amount and substantiality of the material used in relation to the copyrighted work as a whole" and "effect of the use on the potential market for or value of the work."[3]

Copying substantial portions of a copyrighted work is clearly prohibited, and most computer programs are virtually useless unless the entire program is copied. Producing multiple copies of a software package for use in a library's collection also results in the loss of potential sales of the package and constitutes a copyright infringement. Thus, while it is not entirely clear how the concept of fair use applies to software, most librarians agree that making multiple copies of a software program for educational use is probably not permissible under copyright law.

Although the purchaser of a software program does not have the right to make copies for sale or for presentation to others, there is nothing in the copyright law which prohibits a library (or an individual) from lending a program. In fact, commercial rental libraries exist which offer the opportunity to preview a program for a fee. Software producers rankle at rentals because they are viewed as an inexpensive way for customers to copy instead of purchase programs.

Microcomputer centers in academic libraries might be seen as posing a similar problem for software houses, but they are on sound legal ground for several reasons. As nonprofit educational organizations which do not charge a fee for library loans, they do not constitute a commercial threat to software publishers. As institutions which are highly sensitive to the legal and ethical questions of intellectual property, libraries tend to take a very responsible approach to the formulation of loan policies and procedures in relation to copyright. And finally, libraries are protected from liability for illegal copying that patrons may conduct under Section 108(f) of the Copyright Revision Act of 1976:

108(f) Nothing in this section --

(1) shall be construed to impose liability for copyright infringement upon a library or its employees for the unsupervised use of reproducing equipment located on its premises: *Provided,* That such equipment displays a notice that the making of a copy may be subject to copyright law;[4]

In the case of microcomputer centers, "reproducing equipment" is the microcomputer workstation itself. As long as the equipment displays proper notices, libraries should not be held liable for illegal copying by patrons on unsupervised equipment. Specific recommendations for copyright notification are included in the section below on Policies and Procedures for Software Collections.

The only place the copyright law specifically addresses the question of copying computer software is in Section 117:

117. Limitations on exclusive rights:
Computer programs

Notwithstanding the provision of section 106, it is not an infringement for the owner of a copy of a computer program to make or authorize the making of another copy or adaptation of that computer program provided:

(1) that such a new copy or adaptation is created as an essential step in the utilization of the computer program in conjunction with a machine and that it is used in no other manner, or

(2) that such new copy or adaptation is for archival purposes only and that all archival copies are destroyed in the event that continued possession of the computer program should cease to be rightful.[5]

Clearly the purchaser of a software program has the right to adapt or copy the program if those steps are necessary to utilize it or to make an archival copy. Given the fragility of current storage media, most libraries choose to store the original diskette or tape as an archival backup and circulate a copy. As long as the number of copies in circulation is never greater than the number purchased, this practice should meet the requirements of the copyright law.

The clarification provided by Section 117 is helpful, but it leaves many questions unanswered. In addition, most software publishers are not satisfied with the copyright law and seek protection under contract law. The resulting "contract," "user agreement," "license," or "nondisclosure agreement" often includes conditions on the use of the software which are much more restrictive than those of the copyright law itself.

Contract Law and Software Licensing Agreements

Vendors of microcomputer software seek protection through bodies of law other than copyright in part because copyright law lags far behind evolving technology. Commonly a software publisher will register new releases with the Copyright Office, secure trademark registration, and affix a legally binding "contract" or "license" to each software package. The package typically contains a registration card to sign and return to the publisher. By signing the registration card, the user qualifies for customer support but also agrees to the vendor's conditions on the use of the package. To protect themselves against buyers who fail to return the card, the fine print will often claim that by removing the shrink wrap or opening the package the buyer has given tacit agreement to the terms of the contract.

The motivation behind these practices is understandable: software development is expensive, copying is easy, and the publisher wishes to protect its investment and assure profits. Nevertheless, the restrictions have serious implications for libraries. While libraries must take these "box-top" or "shrink-wrap" licenses seriously, they cannot accept them at face value without abrogating rights fundamental to the operation of a library microcomputer center.

A software license typically claims that the manufacturer, not the buyer, owns the program purchased; that the buyer is in fact leasing the program; that the buyer alone is authorized to use it; and that the program may only be run on a single computer in a single location.

The concept of ownership is central to questions of rights of use and duplication of software. When "purchasing" a software package covered by a license, one is, legally speaking, leasing. Technically, one does not own such software but buys the right to use it under the conditions stipulated in the license. The buyer is technically the only licensed user.

The National Commission on New Technological Uses of Copyrighted Works (CONTU) originally recommended to Congress that the provisions of Section 117 of the Copyright Act be accorded to the rightful "possessor" of a copy of a program. But the law as passed states that the owner of a program is granted the limited copying and adaptation privileges specified in Section 117. This may seem a legal technicality, but it leads directly to the question of whether the rights granted under the copyright law are negated by the more restrictive provisions of a software license.

An example of this conflict is the right to make an archival copy. It is not clear whether a court would accept as valid a license that sought to limit a library's right to make an archival copy of a program it had purchased for its software library. If the library is leasing the package, however, and is thus not the "owner," it is at least possible that the court would find that copyright law does not apply. Loaning software in a library or microcomputer center presents a similar problem. Nothing in the copyright law precludes loaning a software program, but many licenses limit the use of software to the buyer.

What does the law say about the relationship between contract law, which varies from state to state, and federal copyright law? Unfortunately, the law is not clear. Software users argue that due to preemption under Section 301 of the copyright law, the conflicting license restriction is invalidated. The principle of preemption states that federal copyright law takes precedence over state law that is in direct conflict with it. However, whether or not contract law is equivalent to "state law" in this case is not clear. Section 108(f)(4) of the copyright law states that "Nothing in this section in any way affects ... any contractual obligations assumed at any time by the library or archives when it obtained a copy or phono record of a work in its collections."[6]

Must we honor both copyright restrictions *and* contract or license agreements? The law has not been tested in the courts and no one will be sure until a test case is decided. Although it did not pass, a bill was recently introduced in Congress which would have provided legal support for the practice of loaning software. While reintroduction of the bill is possible, it will probably take years to clarify the legal issues. In the meantime, libraries must take a position and adopt clear, consistent policies and procedures when they establish microcomputer centers.

Clearly many of the restrictions of software licenses are not aimed at libraries and cannot be accepted if the materials are to be included in a software library. The library should state unequivocally, at the time of software acquisition, that vendors should sell materials to the library only if they agree to the library's terms of use. If the library states these terms of use in a written attachment to its check or purchase order, it is in a strong position to argue that the vendor has accepted its conditions through the sale of the software package. Software vendors are inclined to agree to conditions less restrictive than their normal terms for libraries which demonstrate a responsible attitude toward protecting the rights of the authors and publishers. The appendix contains policy statements and license exemptions which Mann Library currently uses for this purpose.

Trade Secret

One type of law which software vendors frequently use is trade secret protection. Under trade secret, vendors may protect items which cannot necessarily be copyrighted or patented for as long as the secret is not generally known. To obtain trade secret protection, one must prove that appropriate measures have been taken to preserve the secret. Registering a program for copyright, depositing copies in the Library of Congress, and mass marketing the product hardly seem the most discreet procedures for keeping a secret, raising questions about the general applicability of trade secret to commercial software.

Trademarks

Trademark protects a company against competitors who would identify their own goods and services in the minds of customers as those of the trademark holder. Trademark can be used concurrently with copyright, patent, and trade secret protection. Though software vendors employ trademark to prevent large-scale commercial piracy and false advertising, it is not of particular importance to library uses of software.

Patent Protection

Many people believe that software is not patentable because the courts have historically been divided on whether or not one can patent a computer program. Recent decisions, however, point toward increasing use of patents to protect software. Although patents are expensive and time consuming to obtain, software producers see them as the most desirable form of legal protection for the following reasons:

1. Patents provide the broadest scope of protection, potentially excluding others from making, using, or selling any product that embodies the central idea of the patented software.
2. Patents provide the only protection against independent development of like software by others.
3. Patents are a visible asset and can aid in obtaining contracts loans, and capital.
4. Substantial tax benefits can accrue from sale or exclusive licensing of patent rights.

Although libraries may eventually have to consider the implications of patent rights for information access, this is not currently an area of major concern.

Hardware- and Software-based Copy Protection Schemes

Even with the protections offered by copyright, contract, trade secret, trademark, and potentially patent law, the software industry is not satisfied. Software-based protection schemes are used to make the copying of a diskette impossible. However, since clever schemes such as Prolock--which requires the use of a "key" diskette--can be decoded, some software publishers have tried more aggressive protection schemes, such as Killer Prolock. These protection mechanisms employ "worms" or "booby traps" that alter the user's operating system and cause damage to data files if an unauthorized copy of a diskette is made.

A less extreme software-based protection scheme involves encoding diskettes with an electronic fingerprint which is uniquely identified with the program file. The program cannot be operated without the corresponding key diskette. The disadvantages for personal computer users are the difficulties in controlling access to the key diskettes and the inconvenience of using them, particularly when programs are mounted on and run from a hard disk.

Such schemes make microcomputing inconvenient to the individual user and extremely awkward for operators of a microcomputer center. Hardware-based copy protection schemes are extremely unpopular with users and are likely to be abandoned by their promoters. It is critical that libraries develop clear, effective loan policies for software collections and work to make software publishers understand and recognize their needs.

POLICIES AND PROCEDURES FOR SOFTWARE COLLECTIONS

What should a library do about loan policies for software collections when confronted by the confusing array of legal protections just outlined? Software producers are willing to sell or lease to libraries--it gives their products excellent exposure--but they are fearful of illegal copying and of borrowing as a substitute for buying. Librarians must work to convince this emerging branch of the publishing industry that we are sensitive to intellectual property concerns and that our loan policies are designed to enforce compliance with copyright laws. This attitude strengthens the position of libraries in negotiating licenses and influences industry practices as they relate to libraries. At the same time, libraries must not hesitate to use their full rights under the law.

In setting loan policies, our library has tried to protect the legitimate interests of software producers, while preserving the flexibility we need to operate a microcomputer center. We first developed a set of operational procedures and policies that achieve a balance between the interests of the library and the software vendor, and then established a procedure for reviewing the terms of new software acquisitions and for negotiating exemptions from limitations that are incompatible with our center's policies. Developing fair and reasonable loan policies and procedures for software collections has not proved as difficult as we feared it might.

The following operational guidelines are consistent with copyright law and have proven effective in our library:

1. Software will be used on Microcomputer Center machines only (Some libraries loan software for use outside the library.)
2. Program diskettes will remain in the Microcomputer Center at all times. Documentation may be checked out on overnight loan.
3. The library will not run more copies of a program simultaneously than it has purchased. Whenever possible, the original distribution diskette is stored as an archival backup and a working copy is loaned.
4. The library posts a prohibition against the copying of software at the loan counter and at every workstation (see Appendix). Each program diskette displays a similar injunction on screen when it boots up (see Appendix). Patrons thus understand that copying is illegal and that they risk their borrowing privileges in the center should they conduct unauthorized copying of programs.
5. Software is loaned only to members of the university community.
6. The library does not loan to our patrons programs designed to defeat copy protection schemes.

These straightforward guidelines are acceptable to nearly all software publishers, reassuring them that illegal copying is minimized in the Microcomputer Center.

Since the terms of many software licenses are unreasonable and clearly not written with libraries in mind, librarians must be prepared to challenge unacceptable limitations on use. As it would be extremely time consuming to negotiate licenses for each software package when trying to build a sizable collection, the most effective procedure is to state your terms at the time of purchase. This is easily accomplished with a form letter that accompanies a university purchase order (see sample in Appendix). The letter should briefly explain the educational nature of the microcomputer center and detail its loan policies. We attach to the letter a statement of library policies on the loan of software (also in Appendix). Together these documents clearly indicate the type of use the software will receive in the Microcomputer Center and the precautions taken to avoid abuse of the vendor's intellectual property rights. In our experience, nearly all vendors are satisfied with these conditions. Those who are not comfortable with our terms respond with a refusal to sell their product or indicate a willingness to negotiate.

A library that supports a software collection should establish procedures for reviewing the license terms of all new software acquisitions. If the conditions outlined in the purchase letter are not accepted by the publisher, the library must be prepared to negotiate or to cancel an order. Should the vendor ship the product but explicitly reject the library's terms of use, the library must initiate further communication with the vendor or return the package.

A broad commitment to this approach may gradually cause the software industry to realize that libraries are sensitive to intellectual property concerns, that our loan policies are designed to enforce compliance with reasonable protections, and that special license agreements should be developed for library software collections.

ONLINE BIBLIOGRAPHIC DATABASES

Microcomputer centers which teach end-users online searching and bibliographic file management must address the legality of downloading, reformatting, storing, and reusing the results of online searches. As with software collections, technology in this area is moving faster than the law. The copyright law as it presently exists was written in response to print media and is inadequate to regulate the use of databases. There are conflicting interpretations of laws that do exist and much uncertainty surrounds the question of which practices are legal, ethical, and safe.

Online databases raise complex issues concerning intellectual property, including that of copyright as it applies to electronic publishing and that of the copyright of bibliographic databases by organizations such as OCLC. These issues are beyond the scope of this section, which is limited to an overview of the following questions: (1) Is the downloading of the results of a computer search of a bibliographic database for the purpose of storing the data in a microcomputer-based personal information file an infringement of copyright? Is it necessary to ask the permission of the database publisher to download in this manner? (2) If this activity is not an infringement, what restrictions apply to the subsequent reuse of the downloaded information?

Since there is no case law to clarify the legal questions, each library must shape its policies and practices based on an understanding of the issue and the pertinent laws, the needs of its patrons, and its own professional judgment. The discussion that follows will provide background on the issues and facilitate debate and consideration. A point of view is developed, but it should not be construed as legal advice, which should be sought from a lawyer.

The Structure of the Online Database Industry

Commercial database services involve three parties: the end-user, the database vendor, and the database producer or supplier. Database vendors, such as BRS and DIALOG, usually do not own the databases they vend. They provide access to databases owned by database suppliers who hold the database copyright and set the contractual terms.

The pricing structure for database services is complex. In its most rudimentary form, end-users pay database vendors for access to a database and search software, and the vendors then pay royalty charges to the database suppliers for the use of the database. In some cases database suppliers must in turn pay royalties to holders of copyrighted information stored in the supplier's database.

The price paid by the end-user for an online search is determined by a variety of factors, including: the telecommunications network used, the vendor chosen, the database(s) searched, the number of citations identified by searches and the amount of information displayed, the number of minutes of online time, the consumption of processor cycles on the vendor's computer, whether search results are printed online or offline, and database vendor charges such as handling and page charges. These cost components fall into three major categories: telecommunications charges, vendor service charges, and database royalty charges. The online industry is concerned that end-users will use downloading to reduce costs in all three categories through the creation of local databases. The result will be a loss of revenue for the vendors and database suppliers. The promise of CD-ROM technology is similarly seen as both an opportunity for and a potential threat to the online industry. The legal questions surrounding fair use of information are critical in that they may influence the way in which technology is employed to distribute machine-readable databases, affect pricing structures, and, in general, determine patterns of information access in the future.

Copyright of Databases

Machine-readable databases are not specifically mentioned in Section 117 of the copyright law. Any copyright protection they enjoy is under the provisions of the Copyright Act of 1976 on public domain compilations and derivative works. As an original compilation of preexisting materials, a database may qualify as "a work formed by the collection and assembling of preexisting material or of data that are selected, coordinated, or arranged in such a way that the resulting work as a whole constitutes an original work of authorship."[7] With compilations it is the selection and arrangement of materials which makes the work original and which is eligible for copyright, not the materials themselves.

Someone other than the owner of the database may hold copyright on the preexisting materials or data which have been organized in the database. For example, the text of the *New York Times* stored in the NEXIS database is copyrighted by The New York Times Co., while Mead Data Central, Inc., holds the copyright on the NEXIS database as a compilation. An important copyright issue for database vendors and suppliers is whether a "copy" of the material that constitutes the database is made at the time the data are input into the computer and become part of the database, or whether a "copy" results only when a user searches the database and retrieves the copyrighted material. The answer to this question determines the activities for which royalties are paid to the copyright holder.

The legal question of what constitutes a copy of machine-readable data remains unresolved. Similarly, the courts have not ruled on what represents reasonable repackaging and reuse of information retrieved from an online database. Common sense and "fair use" would seem to dictate, however, that limited copying rights are accorded to the database user to a degree analogous with the rights established for print materials. An online system displays the results of a search on the monitor of a user's microcomputer and allows printing of this information. It seems only reasonable that these same search results may be stored on a diskette instead of on paper. The researcher's card file of journal citations is a scholarly tradition of long standing and clearly falls within copyright law. By extension, a microcomputer-based version of the same file should not be an infringement of copyright.

Application of the criteria for determining fair use would support this view: the purpose of the copying is for nonprofit educational use, only a small portion of the whole database is copied, and it does not cause economic harm to the copyright holder or affect the potential market for the database.

Database Supplier Terms and Conditions (Contracts)

Since no case law exists to clarify the application of fair use to database information, database suppliers, like software producers, are going beyond the copyright law for protection. As owners of original compilations, suppliers commonly copyright their databases and then proceed to stipulate further restrictions on the use of the database. These terms and conditions are considered to apply "in addition to customer's adherence with copyright laws applicable to database files."[8] A typical statement of terms reads: "No part of the X Database may be duplicated in hard copy or machine-readable form without prior written authorization."[9]

As with many software licenses, a conflict exists between the terms of the license or contract restricting use of a database and the rights accorded to individuals by copyright law. Through a combination of negotiation, legislation, and case law, a clear legal balance will eventually be struck between the needs of database users and the rights of database suppliers. Meanwhile, libraries and other database users must decide how they will approach the question of downloading.

Policy Considerations in Downloading

While some libraries may have formal policies governing downloading by library staff, most handle such matters on a case-by-case basis. If the library devises a blanket policy, it should arrange for review by legal counsel before implementation to consider whether the institution is vulnerable to a suit.

When teaching students and faculty online searching and file management, the librarian must be prepared to offer information on the ethics and legality of downloading. One must avoid giving legal advice or offering hard and fast rules in a field fraught with uncertainty, but the library should be able to present some facts and a conceptual framework that will help patrons make their own decisions about what types of downloading and reuse are legal and ethical.

In the absence of copyright laws specifically covering databases, approaches to downloading range from strict adherence to the extremely restrictive limitations of the vendor's published database contract, to a decision to ignore all restrictions and download for any purpose from any database. Contrary to the fears of some database suppliers, few individuals and, most likely, no academic libraries engage in large-scale, systematic reproduction of downloaded data. While database owners must protect themselves from commercial piracy of their databases, libraries and academic end-users are not a significant threat. Some end-users will write or call for permission, as required in the contracts, to download from a specific database. Database suppliers usually do give their permission to download for legitimate uses.

Another common practice among end-users is to make judgments on fair use copying from databases by using the analogy of copying from a printed version of a database. If copying or a particular reuse of copied material is legal with printed matter under the copyright law, the same copying or reuse could be interpreted as legal with a machine-readable version of the same information, such as a computer database. This conceptual framework provides a simple and reasonable method for determining legitimate uses of downloading. The approach is clearly consistent with the spirit and intent of the copyright law. It is the author's opinion that policy guidelines based on the parallel treatment of print and computerized information are not likely to be challenged by database suppliers. However, it must be stressed that the concept of "fair use" applies only to copyright law, and the fair use doctrine is not directly applicable to contract restrictions. As with microcomputer software (see above), a conflict exists between the rights and privileges assumed by analogy under copyright law and those stipulated by contractual agreement.

If a library provides public-access microcomputers with communications capabilities, patrons may try to use library equipment to download from databases governed by "contract" restrictions. Librarians must therefore be careful to protect their institutions from liability for illegal downloading. We can do this by consistently including factual statements and basic information on downloading in our end-user instruction programs and by prohibiting systematic reproduction of downloaded searches. If a library does decide to allow downloading beyond the terms and conditions of the contracts of database suppliers, a reasonable guideline (in the author's opinion) might be to allow copying which falls within the provisions of the copyright law. Again, it is wise to seek legal counsel before adopting a policy.

What follows is Mann Library's policy statement on downloading from copyrighted databases. In establishing this policy we have focused on microcomputer software and online databases; however, we believe this policy would apply to other formats, such as databases stored on compact disk.

Policy on Downloading from Copyrighted Databases

Many faculty and students wish to store the results of online searches on their own diskettes. While the copyright law has not been widely tested in its application to the downloading of information from online databases, the library believes that the concept of "fair use" of intellectual property applies regardless of format. Thus, it is widely believed, downloading for educational uses is legal, ethical, and proper as long as it meets the statutory criteria for "fair use," which revolve around:

1. The amount and substantiality of the material used in relation to the copyrighted work as a whole.
2. The effect of the use on the potential market for or value of the work.

In determining copyright infringement, each case is decided on its own facts, with the above criteria, among others, used as a gauge for balancing the equities in "fair use." Members of the academic community have a particularly strong interest in respecting intellectual property rights. Therefore, as with photocopying of print materials or the use of quotations and ideas from the works of others, one should exercise sensitivity to the rights of authors and publishers in the downloading and reuse of computerized information.

Examples:

The following instances of copying are clearly allowed under copyright law for print materials and, by extension, for computerized information:

1. Creating a file of bibliographic citations on a specific subject area for personal research purposes, which would represent a microcomputer-based version of the traditional reprint file.
2. Copying a portion of a machine-readable text for scholarly purposes or for classroom use.

Copying (downloading) for commercial purposes and systematic copying which affects the potential market for a work is illegal. Clear cases of copyright infringement include:

1. Downloading a large portion of a database for resale.
2. Systematically downloading portions of a database for distribution to a large group of researchers as a current awareness service.

Note:

Until the laws regulating intellectual property rights for machine-readable information catch up with the technology available, users of such information must rely on common sense and the general guidelines provided in copyright law. Most database suppliers have promulgated written contract statements of terms and conditions, which are claimed to apply in addition to copyright laws applicable to database files. In some cases, these database contracts are highly restrictive and permit no form of downloading without prior permission from the database publisher.

The library and the university are not responsible for copyright infringement by staff, faculty, or students who ignore or exceed the fair use criteria as outlined in this policy and in §107 of the Copyright Revision Act of 1976. The library and the university are not responsible for any legal suits which might result from contested downloading practices or interpretations of the laws as they pertain to downloading by library users.

TRENDS AND ISSUES

The Future of Copy Protection Laws and Practices

The current state of uncertainty and ambiguity over the application of copyright law to emerging information technologies will only improve with new copyright legislation or the development of a significant body of case law which interprets existing legislation. Congress will resist drafting new legislation until its membership has a clearer picture of the long-range impact of computer technology on information transfer. Some argue that the unique qualities of software require unique legislation, combining elements of copyright, patent, and trade secret laws. The Semi-Conductor Chip Protection Act of 1984, though it has no direct application to computer software, represents the first truly new form of intellectual property protection in nearly a century and could be the harbinger of a new form of copyright law covering electronic information.

In Washington, there is a movement afoot to remove the Copyright Office from the Library of Congress (and the legislative branch of government) and to create a new regulatory agency in the executive branch. Such an agency, according to supporters of the idea, would be more responsive to new technologies through administrative law than the Congress can be through the legislative process. Others think Congress is not likely to concur, however, because copyright is a matter of public policy which its membership will guard jealously.

Another current effort to shape the future patterns of access to computer-readable information is the series of lawsuits, mentioned earlier, that ADAPSO is bringing against customers who make unauthorized copies of microcomputer software. ADAPSO is choosing its cases carefully, focusing on large institutions whose personnel systematically make unauthorized copies of mass-marketed software packages. Although these lawsuits bring attention to the problem of corporate copying, they are settled out of court because they involve clear-cut infringements. As a result, ADAPSO succeeds in intimidating all users without actually putting to legal test the important questions that surround microcomputer software.

In the present legal vacuum, libraries must devise policies which reflect their interpretation of the legal, ethical, and practical considerations in software copying and use, and in the way that they treat information stored in online databases. In so doing, libraries can help define the laws and practices of the future. We feel there really is not much risk for libraries in adopting the stance that the rights granted for use and duplication of print materials apply to computer software and databases. In the absence of guidance from Congress in the form of new legislation, we feel the courts are most likely to decide in the favor of the user's right to fair use.

In *Williams and Wilkins v. the United States*, a decision which upheld the application of fair use to photocopying, and in the recent Sony Betamax case, the courts decided, in the absence of congressional guidance, to side with the user of new technologies. A software publisher or database supplier would have a weak case if an alleged infringement was within the limitations of copyright law but outside the limitations of a contract imposed unilaterally by the supplier.

Just as they have been given greater latitude than private business in photocopying, libraries and academic institutions must be given special consideration in handling and using machine-readable information. The library market is not lucrative enough for publishers to risk losing a precedent-setting court case over an alleged library infringement. Despite all the concern over the provisions of the Copyright Act of 1976, no library has been taken to court by a publisher for copyright infringement. As long as policies are well considered and meet the tests of fair use, and as long as libraries are persistent in attempting to negotiate the removal of the kinds of restrictions described in this chapter, libraries have little to fear in handling computerized information in their microcomputer centers in a manner analogous to their treatment of print collections. In fact, librarians have an obligation to society to actively resist the tendency of the software industry and the database vendors and suppliers to severely limit the use of computerized information.

SUMMARY

1. Because information technologies are developing faster than the laws which regulate their use, librarians must set access policies based on interpretations of how existing laws apply to the new technologies, often without the benefit of a body of case law. In devising policies regulating access to information in machine-readable formats, librarians are helping to define the laws and practices of information handling and access that will pertain in the future. Consequently, libraries must make their decisions in the philosophical context of the role of the library in providing free access to information in a democratic society.

2. The software industry is, in one sense, an immature branch of the publishing industry. Librarians can educate software vendors concerning the principles and protocols of dealing in intellectual property. To establish credibility in this mission, librarians should inform themselves on copyright and intellectual property issues and demonstrate a sensitivity to the importance of protecting the rights of authors and publishers. At the same time, librarians should insist on using their full rights under the law.

3. Under copyright law, libraries have a clear legal right to loan software and are protected from liability for illegal copying by patrons as long as unsupervised microcomputer equipment in the library displays proper notices.

4. While the rights of libraries (and individuals) to use and copy software are defined by copyright law, software producers also employ patent, contract, and trade secret law to regulate the use of their programs. The terms of software contracts (licenses) are frequently more restrictive than the rights provided by copyright law. Among the common license restrictions which prove unacceptable to microcomputer centers are: use of one software package on one specified machine only, preventing the making of archival copies through copy-protection schemes, and limiting use of the program to the buyer.

5. While such contractual terms are frequently not aimed at libraries, they may be legally binding if accepted by the library. Therefore libraries must develop clear policies which do not abrogate their rights under the law and must state their terms of use at the time of purchase. A

mechanism for reviewing licenses is needed, with an efficient procedure for negotiating exemptions from limitations inconsistent with library policy.

6. Sample guidelines for software circulation policy are provided in the Appendix. In our library, we limit circulation activity to the premises of the Microcomputer Center and strictly prohibit the copying of commercial program diskettes.

7. The law is not clear on issues of use and reuse of information downloaded from an online database. We argue that the principles of fair use as applied to printed information are applicable to information in machine-readable formats.

Notes

1. See Carlton Rochell's treatment: "The Knowledge Business: Economic Issues of Access to Bibliographic Information," *College and Research Libraries* 46: 5-12 (Jan. 1985).

2. Jennifer Daryl Slack, "Programming Protection: The Problem of Software," *Journal of Communication* 31: 151-63 (Winter 1981).

3. 17 U.S.C. § 107 (1976).

4. 17 U.S.C. § 108(f)(1976).

5. 17 U.S.C. § 117(1976), as amended by Public Law No. 96-517, Dec. 12, 1980, 94 stat. 3028, codified as amended at 17 U.S.C. § 117 (Supp V, 1981).

6. 17 U.S.C. § 108(f)(4)(1976).

7. 17 U.S.C. § 101 (1976).

8. "Database Supplier Terms and Conditions," DIALOG Information Services, Inc. (Jan. 1985).

9. Ibid.

Chapter 6

Organizing a Software Collection: Cataloging and Classification

Mary Ochs

SOFTWARE IN THE LIBRARY'S COLLECTION

The experience librarians have in organizing collections of information is an excellent reason to incorporate a microcomputer center into a library. Who is better prepared than librarians to organize and control a collection of microcomputer software?

The cataloging and processing of software have, however, created many new challenges for technical services departments. At Mann Library, technical services personnel were involved from the beginning in the process of establishing policies and procedures for the Microcomputer Center. Now, the Technical Services Department catalogs all software for the Microcomputer Center's collection and often arranges to have the materials bound. In addition, the exercise of cataloging software, together with the presence of the Microcomputer Center in the building, has led the Technical Services staff to gain expertise in the use of microcomputers.

The initial policy decision, which affects all others related to technical services, concerns the extent to which the software collection will be integrated into the library's general collection. If a library does not consider software part of the general collection, it can comfortably catalog a software collection in a local database, or perhaps in a book catalog similar to the catalogs many libraries maintain for audiovisual materials. As explained in Chapter 3, however, our policy in collection development is to not discriminate against any information resource because of format. We extend this philosophy to cataloging. Although at this time software is not *physically* integrated into the general collection, we add the records for all software packages to the general catalog for the library. This decision led us to follow the national cataloging standards--including *Anglo-American*

Cataloguing Rules, second edition *(AACR2)*, *Library of Congress Subject Headings*, and LC classification--in order that software records mesh with the cataloging for other materials. It is not absolutely necessary that a library follow LC classification for software, but there are many advantages in using all three national standards.

In technical services, as elsewhere, standard procedures that minimize exceptions make training easier and speed the flow of work. The use of standard cataloging practices to catalog software allows a library to exploit the resources of the bibliographic utilities. Shared cataloging saves time with microcomputer software just as it does with monographs. The ability to order catalog cards and the provision of machine-readable records for an online catalog are also real benefits for the library.

Perhaps the most important advantage to the library of using the same procedures and systems for cataloging software as it does for books, however, is the single, comprehensive database that results. Patrons are best served when they can search one tool, the card catalog or online catalog, to find any material the library owns.

RLIN AND A LOCAL DATABASE

When the library began to catalog software, our philosophy of one catalog for all formats was well established. The MARC format for machine-readable data files, unfortunately, was not. MARC for data files became available on OCLC in the fall of 1984, but it was not available on RLIN until September 1985. Because Cornell is a member of the Research Libraries Group and uses its RLIN system for cataloging, the lack of the MARC format presented a problem for the library. Our choice was either to leave the software collection uncataloged until RLIN made the format available or to develop a temporary local cataloging system. We chose to implement a local catalog in spite of the staff time required because bibliographic control was needed immediately. The alternative was to go back later and catalog a well-used, circulating collection--a difficult task no matter what the format of material.

In order to minimize the duplication of effort in recataloging software materials once the MARC format became available on RLIN, we decided to use the MARC fields in designing a local database. The library considered several microcomputer-based database management software packages for the creation of a catalog of software owned by the Microcomputer Center. dBase III was the package which, in our judgment, best accommodated our needs because it supports a memo field which we use with summaries and other notes. Also, dBase III is flexible enough to create several output formats. In addition to establishing a data structure based on the MARC record, Technical Services staff wrote command files which generate catalog copy in the traditional *AACR2* format, to be tagged for input into RLIN, and in an abbreviated format for addition to a printed catalog in the Microcomputer Center.

The printed catalog of software holdings has proved useful, making the staff aware that a local (Microcomputer Center specific) catalog of software is desirable even though the software records now appear in the RLIN database and in the main library catalog. Thus, the Microcomputer Center receives full sets of cards for all software. We have also chosen to continue the dBase III catalog even with the advent of the RLIN MARC format for software because of applications not available through RLIN. The Microcomputer Center staff has used the dBase III catalog, for example to generate lists of software available in the center for faculty use, lists to send to other libraries with an interest in software, and current lists kept at the reference desk. Student employees working from RLIN copy keep the dBase III file current without a significant investment of professional time.

A local online catalog, as planned for the near future at Cornell, should combine the benefits of RLIN cataloging and a local microcomputer-based system. What the library needs for optimal software control is standardization and shared cataloging, together with a local database, the capability of generating lists, keyword searching, and the ability to limit searches by format (for example, to retrieve *software* for the Macintosh owned by the Microcomputer Center).

CATALOGING ISSUES

These, then, are some of the major policy issues we have encountered. Let's turn now to the "nitty gritties" of cataloging software. We have found that the details of cataloging and processing make us more aware of the special problems of software and lead to further decision making. Early on, the software cataloger will discover the joys of the new trade.

In descriptive cataloging, the most interesting problem is the application of *AACR2* to software. Chapter 9, the chapter dealing with machine-readable data files, was written before microcomputers became available, and thus presents a set of rules that do not fully answer the problems of describing microcomputer software. In the mid-1970s, who could have predicted the tremendous explosion in the microcomputer industry, which has led to the widespread use and collection of software in libraries?

In response to the growing need to catalog software and the inadequacy of the original *AACR2* Chapter 9, the American Library Association's Resources and Technical Services Division created a task force on the Descriptive Cataloging of Microcomputer Software. The task force developed guidelines for interpreting Chapter 9 for software which were published by ALA in 1984.[1]

It is not the purpose of this chapter to instruct the reader in the proper descriptive cataloging of software. There are, however, several points of general interest which are unique to software. The MARC format for machine-readable data files contains field 753 for "technical details access." This field does not conform to *AACR2*, but it has been defined to allow access to records by such technical details as machine and operating system.[2] For example, a 753 field of

753 IBM PC$cDOS 2.0.

identifies a software package for the IBM Personal Computer which requires DOS 2.0, and would print on an added entry card as:

IBM PC--DOS 2.0.

The chief source of information for cataloging a piece of software is the "internal title page"--the first screen of a program which contains the name of the package and the publication and copyright information. Finding this title page requires that the cataloger load and run the program. This is "slightly" more time consuming, in most cases, than opening the cover of a book. Software catalogers must familiarize themselves with all the types of microcomputers for which the library purchases software. They must understand program documentation well enough at least to make every program run. Often software must be installed before it can be cataloged because the program on the original distribution diskette cannot be run before someone--whether it be the cataloger or a technician--configures it for a particular hardware environment. This added step can create a diversion in the usual flow of materials through a technical services department. It also adds substantially to the cost of preparing microcomputer software for cataloging and patron use. Obviously, software catalogers also need convenient access to microcomputer hardware.

The writing of systems requirements notes for software is another area of descriptive cataloging which requires computer expertise. A systems requirements note outlines the hardware and software environment necessary to run a particular package. As the software publishing industry becomes more attuned to the needs of libraries that catalog software, publishers may address this problem, but at present the information is usually scattered throughout the program documentation, to be gleaned and organized by the cataloger.

Summaries of program function are a useful addition to software cataloging records. These can be created by the cataloger, or, as is the case in our library, by staff members of the microcomputer facility. Staff who have actually worked with a program can probably write the most informative summary if their time is available.

There are problems in using the bibliographic utilities for software cataloging. We discussed the possibility of placing a note in the RLIN catalog record indicating that software materials do not circulate, in order to eliminate interlibrary loan requests we are not able to support. However, we decided this is not necessary. Instead, requests will simply be returned indicating that the material does not circulate. Second, until a local online catalog is available at Cornell, the Microcomputer Center will need a separate, site-specific catalog. As mentioned above, the library has designated the Microcomputer Center as an RLIN location and will receive a full set of cards for each software package cataloged.

THE SUBJECT CATALOGING
OF SOFTWARE

The subject cataloging of microcomputer software presents a different set of issues and challenges. Choosing subject headings for the "generic" software packages, such as word processors, spreadsheets, or database managers, poses one problem. Although there are headings in the *Library of Congress Subject Headings* for each of these categories of programs, is it appropriate to use "Electronic spreadsheets" for a program that is a spreadsheet, when the heading was created for books about spreadsheets? The situation is analogous to the rule that one does not use the heading "Dictionaries" for a dictionary. Instead, the dictionary receives a language heading, for example "English language--Dictionaries." The question is whether one can catalog a certain tool--be it a spreadsheet or a dictionary--with the heading for works about that tool. Tradition suggests this is not proper, but in order to best serve the users of our software catalogs, it makes sense to use these headings in this nontraditional way. We have done this in our cataloging.

Another dilemma in subject cataloging is whether to use the form subdivision "Computer programs." In an online catalog, this subdivision is unnecessary because other fields in a cataloging record will facilitate the searching of a subfile of software only. However, in a card catalog, the form subdivisions can help organize large files on a certain subject. For example, at Mann Library, a computer program on nutrition would be lost among several drawers of cards. The heading "Nutrition--Computer programs," serves to distinguish this work as an information resource different from all the books on nutrition.

In general, the demands of software cataloging consume professional time. The cataloger must learn a new set of cataloging rules and also master microcomputer hardware and software. The library benefits, nevertheless, in that the software cataloger will become one of the people on the library staff most familiar with the software collection and the operation of microcomputers.

CLASSIFICATION AND SHELVING

The classification of software was one of the most controversial topics we encountered in setting up our Microcomputer Center software library. One of the main purposes of classifying a collection is to facilitate discovery by browsing. Since most software collections are not browsing collections, it could be argued that organizing a collection by a simple accession number would serve the users just as well. In spite of this, we decided to use LC classification to organize the Microcomputer Center collection.

Classification numbers can be extremely useful in collection development. With records for software integrated into the main catalog, software will appear intermingled with all other materials in the library's shelflist, providing a complete picture of the library's holdings in a given subject area. This function of LC classification is not of overwhelming utility with generic packages, but will increase in importance as our collection expands to include more subject-specific software. The classification of software also permits the physical integration of software into the collection. If in the future we no longer need to house our software collection in a separate facility, it will be a simple matter to move all or part of it to the stacks. A third reason for using LC classification is that the system is familiar to our patrons. Users will not have to learn a new numbering system just for software. This is consistent with our overall philosophy that the library should maintain its collection as an integrated whole whenever possible.

The decision to use the LC classification system for software did not end the problems and controversy relating to classification. Because software packages and documentation come in all shapes and sizes, it is difficult to use a sequence of classification numbers to establish shelf order. Some packages come with one page of documentation and could hang in a file drawer; others come with an oversize manual that will not fit on a standard shelf; still others contain diskettes which cannot be copied and are best stored independently of program documentation to increase security. We have tried to work around these idiosyncrasies of software and have developed shelving arrangements which are functioning fairly well. These will be described in more detail in Chapter 7.

We have included physical processing in our attempt to "mainstream" software materials. Well-packaged software follows the same path through Technical Services as do printed materials. After cataloging, software is marked, labelled, and sent to the Microcomputer Center. All manuals receive call number labels, though diskettes are not labelled. Paperback manuals likely to receive heavy use are hard bound with pockets to hold program diskettes. When a software package arrives with minimal documentation, we place it in a pamphlet binder so that it can be shelved in proper call number order. Where copy-protected diskettes are a problem, we may decide instead to use a hanging folder.

Although the library is an ideal location to house and maintain a software collection, it will certainly not be the only site on a university campus that acquires software. At Cornell, many academic departments purchase packages for instruction and research as well as administrative applications. Cornell Computer Services (CCS) has assembled a large collection of microcomputer software that is available to the university community for loan. As a result, our library perceived a need to create a union list of the software held throughout the campus.

At present, we are working with Cornell Computer Services to create such a union list. All software owned by CCS is currently "cataloged" in a database called the Software Index, which is supported on the Cornell mainframe computers under the database management package SPIRES. We have now written a command file under dBase III that reformats our dBase records to the requirements of SPIRES. The reformatted records we will upload to the mainframe for inclusion in this database. A future goal, of course, will be to make all the information in the SPIRES database accessible through the Cornell libraries' online catalog.

THE FUTURE

Just as library processing for other types of materials has changed and evolved over the years, so too will the cataloging and processing of software.

As computer technology evolves and advances, the rules and methods libraries have so carefully devised may become obsolete. Although technological progress has caused libraries to adopt new procedures in the past, computers have quickened the pace of change. Local area networks and file-servers may replace much of the software library that sits on shelves. Will it then still be useful to catalog the collection as we do now? Will a call number be of any use whatsoever?

We have mentioned lack of standardization as a problem with software. Will software publishers respond to the needs of users and catalogers with greater standardization? And what are the implications of the rapid movement of the software industry for libraries? Can catalogers keep pace with the release of version 1.1, version 1.11, version 1.12 ...? Or are new rules needed that treat software differently than traditional format materials?

These are just a few of the questions and issues that arise in trying to organize a collection of software. To reiterate, however, though the material may be different, the skills required are the same. Who better than librarians to organize collections of electronic information, just as they have always organized collections of other information resources.

SUMMARY

1. Software records should be integrated into the general library catalog, based on the philosophy that libraries should not discriminate against an information resource because of its format.

2. Standard cataloging practices allow for the "mainstreaming" of software materials and assure the most convenient transition to other systems in the future.

3. Initially, cataloging machine-readable data files places heavy demands on catalogers because they must become familiar with software and microcomputers, as well as the rules for cataloging a new format. The library does benefit, however, in that technical services professionals gain a valuable knowledge of microcomputers and computing when they begin to catalog these materials.

4. A library may wish to maintain a local catalog of software holdings in a microcomputer facility, in addition to adding these records to its general catalogs. This is particularly true if the library's online catalog does not permit the isolation of software holdings by format.

5. Software should receive subject cataloging, but each library will have to address the dilemmas that surround the assignment of subject headings

to generic applications software. The library's decisions in this area should serve the needs of its patrons.

6. Although many software collections will not be browsing collections, software should be assigned classification numbers to provide for integration into the shelflist and possible future integration into the main collection. Standard classification systems are familiar to library users.

7. A library should physically process software like other materials using binding, labels and markings, pockets, and containers where these are appropriate to the expected use of the material. A library should not underestimate the time needed to properly configure software and to maintain files of master and archival diskettes, however, in that these are special procedures not necessary with traditional format materials.

Notes

1. Committee on Cataloging: Description and Access, Cataloging and Classification Section, Resources and Technical Services Division, American Library Association. *Guidelines for Using AACR2 Chapter 9 for Cataloging Microcomputer Software.* (Chicago: American Library Association, 1984).

2. OCLC. *Machine-Readable Data Files Format.* (Dublin, Ohio: OCLC, 1984).

Chapter 7

Software Circulation and Patron Support

James Madden

After 15 months of development, the Microcomputer Center's software collection contained approximately 75 titles and nearly 250 packages. Of course, several productivity packages quickly became favorites and circulated much more frequently than other software items. In the year ending June 1986, the Microcomputer Center conducted 39,503 loan transactions. The average monthly circulation of 4,350 items during spring semester 1986 showed a dramatic increase over the 1,332 transactions conducted in the center's first month of operation. Software now accounts for approximately ten percent of loan activity at Mann Library.

To support efficiently a software collection that grows rapidly and supports heavy circulation, a library must consider how to shelve the software and how to package materials that require careful handling. As suggested in Chapter 6, while some software is shelved with its documentation, we have found that storing software in hanging floppy diskette folders with minimal documentation--special instructions and reference cards--works best for our facility. Patrons who are familiar with popular software packages rarely use reference manuals. Transparent hanging folders allow an operator to determine, at a glance, whether all borrowed materials--including key diskettes and templates--have been returned.

Program documentation is often not constructed to withstand constant use by library patrons. Therefore, we find it necessary to bind manuals that we believe will receive heavy use. Documentation that is less likely to circulate frequently and documentation that we anticipate will be updated frequently are, in most cases, shelved in their original packaging.

For each software package the Microcomputer Center places on its shelves, we make entries in three files--a file of master diskettes, a file containing information about the package's operation, and a file of information pertaining to purchase, registration, and any special licensing arrangements with the software vendor. In addition, we seek to archive original distribution diskettes, as received from the vendor, whenever possible.

Program diskettes are not useful until we have configured them for our hardware, a process requiring about two hours of a specially trained student operator's time. The file of master diskettes insures that we do not lose the results of this configuration work. The program diskettes in this file, which do not circulate, allow any member of the center's staff to quickly repair circulation diskettes that have been altered without repeating the configuration process. Occasionally, copy-protection schemes do not allow us to create a useful master copy; these packages must be dealt with on a case-by-case basis.

As our collection grows, it becomes increasingly difficult for any one staff member to learn the intricacies of each piece of software, making the file containing information about each package a valuable resource. When patrons pose new questions about the operation of a software package, or our student operators unravel some facet of its behavior, we add to this file. Operators may then refer to the file, which represents in effect our accumulated knowledge about the operation of the software in our collection, when they encounter software problems that they have not experienced before.

The file of purchase information and licensing arrangements we use primarily for administrative purposes. It is our record of the library's relationship with each software house from which we purchase programs. In most cases, the file contains only copies of program registration cards, but it may hold correspondence that traces a negotiation with the vendor.

In many respects, the circulation of software within the Microcomputer Center resembles circulation at the library's reserve desk. Materials are loaned on a short-term basis for use on the premises. The Microcomputer Center loans software for a period of one hour. If someone else is not waiting for a package at the end of this period, the patron may go on using it. We do not let patrons take software out of the center, though we do allow people to check out documentation for reading elsewhere. Our policy for borrowing materials overnight is consistent with that of the reserve desk. Users may check materials out one hour before the center closes. These materials must be returned within an hour after the time the center opens on the following day. Otherwise, the patron is fined.

Software does raise problems that are not encountered at the reserve desk. While patrons who appear at reserve are typically able to read, many people who borrow software lack confidence in their ability to use a microcomputer. Microcomputers and software generate many questions, especially when their behavior does not meet the user's expectations. Software is a fragile medium which requires constant maintenance in a public-access environment. In addition, the center must support microcomputer hardware and peripherals with all their associated maintenance and technical problems.

THE SOFTWARE RESERVE COLLECTION

As noted in Chapter 3, the Microcomputer Center supports a reserve collection of software in addition to its permanent collection. This section will treat the software reserve collection, while the next will discuss current patterns of use for the standing collection.

The reserve collection consists primarily of software packages placed by faculty members of the library's constituent colleges who are having students use microcomputers in their courses. In most instances, the software is subject-specific. Over the last two academic semesters, for instance, we have handled a BASIC program that simulates the growth of deer populations, a financial accounting program for use in agricultural economics, a diet analysis program, and a guided instruction package entitled "Psychology and Life," among others. A number of these programs have been written by the faculty members whose courses they support.

Reserve software is a transient presence in our collection, but it poses all the problems of "full-time" additions to our holdings. We must insure that each package is properly configured to run on our microcomputers and to drive our printers. When student patrons encounter difficulties with software they expect assistance--that the package is reserve software makes no difference if the patron cannot get the program to work. As it is even more difficult for student staff to be conversant with reserve software than with our permanent collection, we make every effort to see that professors include adequate documentation and tutorial materials with their reserve placements.

When the Microcomputer Center opened in the spring of 1984, there was no precedent at Cornell for "course reserve software." In those computer science courses which required the use of particular software packages to provide programming environments, students had been responsible for bringing software with them to the machine. This has changed as microcomputing has grown more pervasive in the Cornell curriculum, and as professors have begun to use a broader spectrum of software in their teaching. At this time (October 1986), reserve software loans can run as high as 20 percent of our circulation in a given week. The particular packages in heavy use, of course, vary with course assignments.

In order to control reserve activity, the library has formulated a set of written guidelines for distribution to faculty members. These policies are consistent with those we have developed in the past to control reserve placements. A copy is included in the Appendix.

THE PERMANENT COLLECTION–
POINTS OF ENTRY TO COMPUTING

Some observers of shifts in the student scene classify the 1980s as the decade of nascent "yuppies." People who trace trends in microcomputing perhaps think of the 1980s as the beginning of the word-processing era. In the library, we associate the decade with the birth of a new information age, but we must admit that word processing remains the most common use of the microcomputer on a college campus. The late night "tap, tap...bing" that so many of us remember from our college years has given way to the clicking of keyboards and the metallic whine of printers.

Word processing is the introductory point for many novices in the computer world. A growing number of courses in our constituent colleges now require the use of word processing, in order that students can revise their work when necessary. With the ease of use of current generation word-processing systems, the opportunity to make revisions easily, the availability of spelling checker programs, and a long list of other features, students can produce high-quality documents with less time and trouble than ever before. Most patrons who learn to use microcomputers to write their papers find it hard to believe that they survived with just a typewriter before discovering the wonders of word processing.

The use of a microcomputer for word processing is a skill which students can build upon in learning to use computers for sophisticated information management applications. As a result, our instructional program includes a series of introductory word-processing workshops each semester. At this time, word-processing activity on the machines in the Microcomputer Center is not restricted. Within the next year, however, we may find it necessary to limit the number of word-processing software packages available for loan, in order to accommodate other uses of the microcomputer.

After familiarizing themselves with a word-processing package, microcomputers, and the environment of the Microcomputer Center, patrons begin to explore other applications of computers. While some people stumble upon useful packages by perusing the software collection out of curiosity, others systematically identify areas where a microcomputer could assist them in completing a project. Often these patrons will describe their project to one of the center's staff members and seek advice on which packages would be most appropriate for their needs. Spreadsheets and database management programs represent the types of applications that users most frequently explore following a positive experience with a word-processing system. First-time users are also likely to investigate the capabilities of several computers. For example, a patron who learns to use a word processor on the IBM PC might wish to produce an illustrative chart, which could most easily be created on the Apple Macintosh.

Unless patrons have extremely bad experiences in learning to use a word-processing package, such as losing a 30-page document at 11:30 on the night before the paper is due, their expertise in using both the word processor and other software will grow. In most cases, even the most frustrated patrons make more than one attempt to work productively at a microcomputer. Once you've tried it, you're hooked.

Although most patrons first learn to use computers for word processing, some gain their initial exposure to microcomputers through course-related applications. Others approach microcomputers from a programming background. Students involved in computer science courses can usually learn applications packages with little difficulty. Other students are introduced to microcomputers through the library's online searching workshops.

Any academic library that establishes a microcomputer center will find itself surrounded by an existing campus software environment that is peculiar to the institution, in some respects. The campus computing center will have chosen to support certain software packages, which then become the "default" choice throughout the university, or the computer science department may use specific software applications in its courses. The challenge is to support existing patron computing and, at the same time, to influence software choices in a creative way. Because of the difficulty of retraining a whole community of users, packages that will see wide use should be carefully evaluated before selection. Given the rate at which new software is produced and the level of activity in our facility, we cannot always integrate sophisticated new applications into the Microcomputer Center's collection the moment they are released. We usually introduce new software packages that will be widely used and upgraded versions of popular packages at the beginning of an academic semester, giving us a chance to familiarize our student operators with the software and to prepare informational handouts for patrons.

WordPerfect, as the most widely supported word-processing package at Cornell, is our most heavily circulated software item. Lotus 1-2-3 has been the most popular spreadsheet package and also the second most heavily circulated item. Recently, however, as our patrons become increasingly sophisticated with microcomputers, we have observed a marked increase in the variety of packages circulated daily. Some of our reserve materials become the most popular software packages for the brief periods immediately preceding assignment deadlines.

Patrons are beginning to build personal databases with several of our database management packages. Growing numbers of researchers are exploring our extensive collection of bibliographic management software. Veteran users have learned to analyze packages for their strengths and weaknesses and to select packages that are best suited to a given application.

Other items that circulate frequently fall into a category that we might call "odds and ends." This category encompasses operating system diskettes, temporary data storage diskettes for patron use, utility diskettes for maintaining and recovering files, diskettes that enable a patron to utilize a printer's special features, and diskettes that create exceptionally large printing buffers. This collection of diskettes continues to grow in response to problems which patrons encounter regularly. For example, patrons who wish to print large spreadsheets can borrow a diskette that from a batch file automatically sets the printer for condensed print and creates a large memory buffer, allowing the printer to keep pace with output from their computers. This is a local solution to a local problem, which might not work on someone else's hardware configuration.

Our collection includes tutorials that introduce patrons to the operation of microcomputers and to several of our more popular software packages. These are useful when a patron wants to learn a new applications program, or when users tell us that they have never used a microcomputer before and just want to get started. Because our manuals often circulate separately from the folders that contain diskettes and because veteran users rarely refer to them, program documentation might also be added to the category of miscellaneous circulation items.

THE SPECTRUM OF MICROCOMPUTER CENTER PATRONS

Several semesters of operation have given us insights into the spectrum of personalities to expect among our patrons. Without stretching the truth too far, we can say that users fall into four general categories that can be defined by the amount of support they require from the center's staff. In the best of all possible worlds, all patrons would fall into the category of comfortable users. These patrons are patient and competent; they understand that, in the computer world, expected results are not usually obtained from a first attempt. They are willing to experiment and their occasional questions are legitimate and interesting.

The second category consists of patrons who are genuinely interested in learning about computers but somewhat hesitant to experiment. These people accept the fact that they may not achieve their project goals immediately and they usually learn from their mistakes. Although their questions are frequent and often routine, it is clear that these patrons are developing an understanding of microcomputers and that they will eventually apply this knowledge to overcome barriers independently.

The third group of patrons would convince any observer that Microcomputer Center employees earn their money. These students are not interested in learning about microcomputers. In their perception, software is like a lawnmower--you buy it at a shopping mall and then pay the kid next door to mow the lawn. Their only concern is completing an assignment that was due fifteen minutes ago or obtaining a printout that must be delivered to the thesis secretary before they catch a plane out of town in an hour. In these situations, patrons are easily frustrated by unsatisfactory results. They expect the center's staff to resolve their problems instantly and, in short, pose a potential threat to the hardware.

Perhaps the most difficult group of patrons to serve, however, are those who know they must use a microcomputer to complete their project but refuse to believe that they will ever be able to master its operation without a consultant sitting next to them at all times. "Paranoid" is the term that best describes this category of user. Because their understanding of computers is minimal, they develop superstitions about the operations of a microcomputer. They may insist on using the same machine they did yesterday or refuse to use copy 17 of a program because they imagine it to have done them wrong.

These patrons are usually the most demanding, not because they are innately aggressive, but because they feel threatened by unfamiliar technology. The barrage of repetitive questions is seemingly endless. In the end, though, these patrons are grateful for the support they obtain from the center's staff. Some even bring peace offerings or write letters of thanks. We accept the peace offerings even though food is not allowed in the Microcomputer Center. Occasionally these patrons overcome their "computer-phobia" and move to one of the first two categories--usually the second.

SOFTWARE CONSULTATION

As is by now obvious, patrons who borrow software frequently need assistance to use the materials the library has loaned them. To address this concern, we train all members of the Microcomputer Center's staff to assist patrons in identifying appropriate packages for their applications. In addition to helping patrons select software, the staff of the center spends much time answering questions about the operation of software packages. Sometimes a student operator can answer a patron's question at the loan counter or upon brief examination of the patron's screen. Frequently, simply handing the patron a manual or suggesting the review of a certain section of software documentation is a satisfactory response.

On the other hand, problems that we cannot resolve quickly also arise. Occasionally, the only copy of a valuable file will be scrambled or someone will ask for help configuring a software package of their own to work with one of our printers. Questions of this type can take several hours of staff time to resolve. Often we ask the patron to come back when the center is less busy and a staff member can devote a block of time to the problem, or when a staff member with an extensive understanding of the package in question will be on duty. When our staff lacks the expertise to answer a question, we can usually refer the patron to a person on campus who can help solve the problem. To meet this need, we maintain notebooks and files of information about the services of Cornell Computer Services and other campus computing organizations.

Soon after the center opened we realized that our staff was answering the same questions over and over again. In the interests of efficiency and our state of mind, we decided that time invested in preparing handouts addressing these chronic concerns is time well spent. Our handouts include instructions on such matters as formatting diskettes, using WordPerfect for the first time, and logging on to Cornell's mainframe computers. We also have schedules of workshop offerings, applications for student staff positions, classroom reservation information sheets, software request forms, and forms for reporting defective software packages or hardware devices. A thorough collection of handouts smooths the operation of the center because it offers a quick, satisfying response to a large number of questions asked at the circulation counter.

The sophistication of our patrons has increased dramatically since the Microcomputer Center opened. We have seen a drop in the use of "tutorial" programs, which review the operation of a microcomputer, and in the need for our student operators to offer initial "hand-holding" support. The majority of our patrons now execute routine operations easily and have a working knowledge of the software packages they use most frequently.

It would seem that the burden of providing consulting support to users should lighten as patrons grow more sophisticated. In fact, this is only partly true. Patrons may bring us fewer questions than when they began computing, but when they do have a question it is more likely to involve a complex point that we have not encountered before. To stay ahead of the patron in software expertise, the Microcomputer Center will need to foster further specialization among the members of our student staff. For consultation on advanced software problems, we may have to request that the patron return when our resident "expert" is scheduled to work on the Microcomputer Center desk.

Despite the advances patrons have made in their understanding of microcomputers, certain characteristics of our clientele will not change. Student users will continue to face academic pressures. They will continue to experience frustration when working with unfamiliar technology. And they will expect--and sometimes appreciate--assistance from the nearest library staff member.

SECURITY AND CIRCULATION CONTROL

Two of the greatest security concerns we dealt with in planning the day-to-day operation of the Microcomputer Center were controlling access to telecommunications and insuring that the software we loan comes back in good order. Part of our program for the Microcomputer Center was the support of patrons who wish to conduct searches of online databases, so we had to equip several of our machines with modems. As a modem attached to an unrestricted line is essentially a telephone that can dial any number in the world, the library must take steps to prevent abuse. When our search stations will not be in use for an extended period, we remove the cords that connect the modems to our telephone jacks. Furthermore, the machines containing modems are located next to the staff area. Modems produce a distinctive noise when dialed which makes it difficult for a patron to use the modem without drawing the attention of staff members, who are trained to investigate this activity. As outlined in Chapter 9, at this time online searches are conducted with a library staff member present to coach users of the search service. It is the responsibility of this individual to determine that the library will receive compensation for search costs, through direct payment or through a course subsidy.

Libraries have struggled with the problem of efficiently securing the return of their books for years. A software collection adds several new twists. The Microcomputer Center currently conducts approximately 4,500 software loans each month, making it impossible to examine thoroughly each package when it is returned. The library must rely on thoughtful packaging, attentive operators, and a high level of trust. We designed the center so that everyone has to enter and exit past the circulation desk. An alarm sounds if anyone exits through the rear emergency door. To date, the center has lost only a few software packages.

All materials, including diskettes and keyboard templates, are stamped to identify them as library property. Every program diskette in our collection contains a batch file that flashes messages on the computer screen, informing patrons of the Microcomputer Center's conditions of use and reminding them that the software belongs to Mann Library. Patrons suspected of violating these guidelines or other library policies are confronted and dealt with appropriately.

The Microcomputer Center controls software circulation with a locally developed monitor program. The program, originally written by one of the center's student employees shortly after we opened, has since gone through two major modifications, each planned before attempts were made to modify the BASIC code. We have discussed the possibility of using the circulation component of the Cornell libraries' integrated library system when that system becomes available. While this would offer advantages in the control of software circulation, it would force us to forego our current ability to monitor the use of workstations within the center. The Information Technology Section will give this question further thought as the integrated library system is implemented.

All patrons who come into the center must first check in at the loan counter. The operator collects their ID cards and logs them onto the "monitor," which runs on an IBM PC located on a corner of the loan desk. If a patron borrows software (many patrons bring their own software), the operator also enters this transaction. Once a patron has been logged in, the monitor program keeps track of the length of time the patron has been working. This allows the operator to determine quickly which patron has been working the longest time in excess of one hour, in order to make workstations available to patrons who are waiting for machines when the Microcomputer Center is busy. At check-out time, the monitor lists the packages a patron has borrowed on screen, so the operator can verify they have been returned. The program also maintains a list of people waiting to use workstations. A utility program generates summary usage and circulation statistics each day from a transaction file produced by the monitor program. We then use these figures to prepare monthly reports under Lotus 1-2-3.

SOFTWARE MAINTENANCE

In addition to insuring that all software stays in the center, we strive to keep all packages in good working order. Although we train patrons to use software properly in our instructional program, it is unrealistic to expect everyone to be aware of all of the correct procedures for using materials in our collection. We would be extremely pleased if patrons did not make the same mistake twice, but experience has taught us to be somewhat less than optimistic.

Microcomputer software is transient: it can be modified or even erased by the patron without any visible indication that this has happened. With some software packages, if a patron does not properly exit a program at the end of a work session the next user may encounter problems. A software library therefore must have a mechanism for repairing damaged program diskettes. As mentioned above, we have established a file of master copies of working diskettes for each package in our collection. Each diskette in this file is properly configured for the monitors, disk drives, and printers in our center and flashes the appropriate warnings about copyright and copying on screen. These diskettes do not circulate; they are used only to repair defective circulation copies.

While the cost, in both diskettes and staff time, to maintain this collection is high, the file is essential to our operation. The collection of master working copies saves considerable effort because the procedure for repairing a diskette that misbehaves is the same for each package in our circulating collection--operators simply have to copy the master working diskette. Without this file, we would have to repair each diskette by reformatting the defective diskette, placing the operating system on the diskette, copying all necessary files from a back-up copy, adding files which are required for operation in our facility, and creating an appropriate batch file for start-up.

Within the next year we hope to install a file-server to help manage the circulation of software within the center. A file-server is a storage device, supported by a local area network, that would make a bank of program files available to any workstation in the facility and eliminate the need to distribute diskettes for our most popular programs at the loan counter. This system has distinct advantages over our present system of circulating software. Because we would no longer have to circulate diskettes for many packages, security concerns would be reduced and physical damage to program diskettes would occur less frequently than it does under the current system. If a program were established as a "read-only" file on the file-server, patrons would not be able to modify program files inadvertently, as they can on diskette.

CONSISTENCY WITH OTHER CAMPUS COMPUTER FACILITIES

Because of its central location, extensive software collection, consulting support, and pleasing aesthetics, the Microcomputer Center is popular among students. However, it is only one of many locations where students have access to microcomputers on the Cornell campus. As stated in Chapter 1, even within the library's two sponsoring colleges--Agriculture and Human Ecology--there are three other large facilities. Cornell Computer Services also administers several microcomputer centers. Students use microcomputers in laboratories, their academic departments, and, increasingly, in their dormitory rooms. Because ours is not the only computer center on campus, we must be aware of the operation and programs of other facilities and maintain as much consistency with them as is practical.

Whenever possible we maintain software compatibility with the other facilities on campus. Patrons are usually not aware of the dangers of using different versions of a software package, or of working with two releases of an operating system, until their files have been extensively damaged. While the responsibility for such frustrating experiences should perhaps be borne by patrons who ignore warnings about incompatibility, the library does well to head off such disasters. Inconvenience for the patron means bad publicity for the library, and the staff time required to repair a patron's damaged file will, in the end, come out of the library's operating budget.

An awareness of the programs of other centers at Cornell aids us in serving our patrons most effectively. We can refer patrons to facilities that have the hardware or software they require, or to a consultant with the expertise necessary to solve a particularly difficult problem. It does not make sense to duplicate work done by other campus organizations in structuring a workshop or preparing written materials designed to assist users in their attempts to use new software. We trade these resources whenever possible.

Cooperation among centers provides a computing environment that, though it may not be uniform, is at least not capriciously various. This is an important consideration as academic computing moves to microcomputers. Without a university mainframe to impose consistency, there is a real danger that "the center will not hold." At Cornell, with its diverse curriculum and decentralized administrative structure, the cooperation needed to achieve some reasonable consistency tends to be informal and often takes place at a junior level. The different organizations involved in microcomputing do consult, however, and the result is of benefit to the user. On some campuses, there may be potential for the library to serve as a mediating agency in this sort of undertaking.

TRENDS AND PROJECTIONS

The level of computer use and software loan activity in the Microcomputer Center continues to increase. Waiting lists are no longer unusual and patrons try to work efficiently while they have access to a machine. Heavy use, though it may place a strain on the staff, is, of course, welcome. Still, the capacity of the center to support patrons is limited by the number of microcomputers available. More faculty members are beginning to place course-related software packages on reserve in the center. As a result, patrons who might not otherwise have had an interest in microcomputers come to complete course assignments. After this initial exposure, many continue to make use of computers for their own purposes.

As suggested above, when we opened the Microcomputer Center for business in the spring of 1984, our audience had a great deal of interest in microcomputing but little experience. Now most of our patrons are reasonably sophisticated. In the first months, on-screen tutorials and basic applications packages represented most of our circulation. This is changing. A much wider variety of software passes over our circulation counter, reflecting new diversity in the ways students and faculty members put microcomputers to work. Microcomputing is exercising an ever larger influence on the academic curriculum, and more students are coming to college with some background in computing, if not in programming. We are pleased to think that the library's programs of instruction, discussed in detail in Part 3, have played some role in the transformation we have observed.

Mann Library does have a specific "angle" on microcomputing. We are most interested in supporting the use of microcomputers as tools that permit one to access information, retrieve the information needed, and then control that information locally. We currently make little effort, however, except in our instructional program, to favor any particular type of microcomputer application. As time goes on, we may find it necessary to develop policies that favor the activities we feel are central to the mission of the library, over other sorts of computing. The use of "generic" microcomputer applications would then tend to migrate to other computer facilities on the Cornell campus.

SUMMARY

1. The Microcomputer Center is among the library's busiest public access points. Software must be carefully organized and packaged to accommodate heavy circulation. Staff members must be prepared to answer a broad variety of questions about microcomputer applications. An efficient reference file is helpful in this regard as a software collection grows.

2. In an academic setting, a "reserve" software collection is a valuable service which the library may choose to provide to students and faculty through its microcomputer center. The difficulty with reserve software is that microcomputer center staff members experience high short-term demand for packages with which they are not familiar. Reserve software presents all the configuration problems of the regular collection, in a compressed time frame.

3. Most novices learn about microcomputers through word processing. Once patrons are comfortable with a microcomputer they often proceed to explore other applications. Although the library does not discourage any use of a computer, other than game playing and illegal copying of program diskettes, our programs and software collection emphasize the use of a microcomputer for information access and retrieval, and for the local control of retrieved information.

4. The burden of patron support in our Microcomputer Center is carried by a staff of student assistants. We place great emphasis on training these operators to assist patrons with software and hardware problems. The Microcomputer Center work is attractive to students, allowing us to select a group of skilled and motivated operators. Students with programming skills can be a valuable resource to the library itself, as staff make increasing use of microcomputers.

5. Patrons often progress through identifiable stages of understanding, each requiring varying levels of staff support, as their expertise in computing develops. Microcomputing remains a complex and often frustrating technology for the user, meaning that a library must expect to dedicate staff resources to patron support if it plans to open a microcomputer facility.

6. Because of the cost of software and the nature of the restrictions that govern its use, a library must carefully monitor the circulation of diskettes and documentation. Software must be kept in good working order, again requiring a commitment of staff time. Staff must also account for charges incurred in using workstations to access remote databases.

7. The library should seek to maintain compatibility between its computer facility and other similar facilities on a university campus whenever possible.

8. As the body of capable microcomputer users at Cornell continues to grow, we will tailor the program of our Microcomputer Center to better address the information needs of the library's patrons. Given current pressures on public computing facilities, a library should consider what spectrum of activities it will actively support.

Part 3

Information Retrieval and Management:

Teaching the User

Chapter 8

Overview of Instructional Programs

Howard Curtis and Joan Lippincott

"LIBRARY INSTRUCTION" IN AN INFORMATION SOCIETY

It is widely argued that for the economies of the developed nations, information is rapidly growing more important than even the natural resource base. Information itself has become a strategic resource, and in its efficient control lies the means to social productivity. Workers and citizens in this emerging "postindustrial" society will need the skills to find and manipulate information on the job and in their private lives to a degree that has not been true in the past. While trends such as "telecommuting" may or may not change the places where we work, an increasing proportion of the population will work more frequently and more intensely with information than ever before. These developments present libraries with important challenges and opportunities.

Our library views instruction as a major mission and responsibility. The need for expanded and technically advanced instructional facilities was a central reason for building the Microcomputer Center. We use a broad definition of the proper place and function of library instruction. At the same time, we are conservative in asserting that at base libraries are in the same business they have always been in: they collect sources of information, they store and organize information, they support mechanisms of access to information, and they provide instruction and consultation to patrons in methods of accessing, retrieving, and controlling information. What has changed in the past decade is the power and sophistication of the technologies that society employs in the control of information. Thus, a library need not radically redefine its role in order to offer instruction in computer-based information systems. Indeed, if a library fails to develop such a program of instruction, it is not only missing an opportunity to expand its role in academic life and its influence on the university information environment, it is actually relinquishing a traditional function.

The Scope of a Library Program in "Information Literacy"

As a result of the increasing importance of information in society, the scope of the instruction that libraries can and should offer has expanded in recent years. "Library instruction" or "bibliographic instruction," terms used interchangeably in the profession, can include a wide variety of activities. As programs of library instruction gained momentum during the 1970s, librarians shifted away from emphasizing particular tools and began to teach patrons to formulate a "search strategy" to locate information. Some library instruction classes include discussions of the publication process in academic disciplines, the evaluation of materials, specific citation formats, and methods of locating information in the community.

For years, library professionals have also introduced online databases in their instructional programs, but they have usually treated these databases as a peripheral resource, due to the need for an intermediary and the cost of most online searching. The exception has been found in efforts to teach users the intricacies of online catalogs, and, in very recent years, in a growing movement toward teaching people to search user-friendly commercial online database systems.

Philosophically, we choose not to draw a sharp distinction between teaching automated systems and teaching manual methods of information access, retrieval, and control. These constitute two separate vehicles, not two separate ends. As was seen in Part 2, our library stresses the importance of access to and organization of information in whatever format it exists. This principle applies not only to the collections of the library but also to the skills with which we seek to equip our student and faculty patrons.

For much the same reason that we do not distinguish strongly between automated and manual methods of locating and managing information, the library does not limit its scope to bibliographic information. By tradition and professional training, librarians are expert in the control of bibliographic data, and we certainly seek to extend that expertise to the automated environment. This is a major justification for our program of instruction in "bibliographic file management," described in Chapter 11, and for our consulting activities in the area of small database design and construction. Nevertheless, the library by no means restricts its instructional programs to bibliographic access and control. We are trying to position ourselves within the university to teach our patrons to access, retrieve, and control the information that they need in their research or that they will need in their careers. For a library that pursues this goal, the terms "bibliographic instruction" and "library instruction" are too narrow to describe properly the scope of its instructional program. We prefer the idea that the library undertakes instruction in "information literacy" within the university.

What a library can achieve in the short term as a teaching organization is of course constrained by the human and financial resources available. Still there is every reason for the library to take a broad view of what library personnel should teach. Although we continue to offer traditional bibliographic instruction, our teaching programs in accessing and controlling information with a computer have grown rapidly in the last three years and have attracted considerable attention at Cornell. Because this section of the book focuses on the relationship between a library microcomputer center and library instruction, we will concentrate here on the computer side of instruction in our library.

Integrating Instruction into the Academic Curriculum

Unless a library develops a coherent plan for teaching about information at various levels in the curriculum, there will be no way to assure that all students are exposed to this important area of study. At the same time, convincing administrators and faculty members that developing an understanding of how information is organized, retrieved, and managed should be an integral component of all students' academic experience may not be an easy task.

The library, of course, can develop its own stand-alone program of instruction, but most professionals involved in library instruction do not favor this approach. Librarians need to work with administrators, curriculum committees, and individual faculty members to integrate learning about information into the academic curriculum. Promoting a course-related or course-integrated program has several benefits: students learn about information sources in conjunction with an assignment and therefore consider the material relevant; the library can utilize subject-specific sources, introducing students to important resources in their particular fields of study; and, by working closely with faculty, librarians can better assess the needs of their student clientele.

THE INSTITUTIONAL ENVIRONMENT

Every academic library functions within particular institutional surroundings. At some universities, librarians enjoy faculty status and teach credit-bearing courses within the regular curriculum. In other institutions, library instruction lies outside the course structure, consisting entirely of workshops, tours, and term paper clinics. Another important question on any campus today is that of how library instruction is related to instruction offered by personnel of the computing center. The following represents a brief summary of how things stand at Cornell.

Library Instruction

As with many programs and services on the Cornell campus, library instruction is decentralized. Each library in the system develops its own program to reach its own clientele. Programs range from that of the undergraduate library, which makes an effort to reach liberal arts students in a wide variety of subjects and at many levels, to those of some of the smaller libraries which consider individualized reference service to constitute their instructional program. There is no general library instruction program for freshmen, nor does the library offer credit courses, except in some specialized disciplines such as law and music. The majority of library instructional activities are course related or course integrated. During 1984-85, the libraries at Cornell taught a total of 688 classes reaching 11,313 participants. Of those, Mann offered 254 with attendance of 4,862.

Efforts are made to communicate about library instruction activities on campus through a Working Group on Library Instruction, which includes representatives from all libraries. This group has also collaborated on promotional materials, guides and handouts, and professional development activities.

The majority of library instruction classes at Cornell emphasize the development of a logical search strategy for finding information in print sources. Online databases are mentioned but not emphasized. The law library instructs its students in the LEXIS system and one other campus library has experimented with end-user instruction on a limited basis.

Computer Services Instruction

Cornell Computer Services (CCS) is one of three large administrative units at Cornell that offer significant programs of instruction outside the structure of the college curricula, the others being the libraries and the university personnel office. Whereas the Department of Computer Science teaches credit courses in the theory and practice of programming, in machine organization and logic, and in other aspects of the academic field of computer science, Computer Services offers workshops designed to assist the user in fully utilizing the university's computing resources.

As was mentioned in the Introduction, although CCS has provided this instructional service for at least the past five years, the nature of its offerings has changed dramatically with the introduction of microcomputers. Whereas in 1981, CCS's program of workshops concentrated on the Cornell mainframes, more than half its offerings now have to do with microcomputers and microcomputer software. The trend toward decentralized computing support described in the Introduction paralleled this transformation in the content of workshops.

Although our library does teach some workshops in standard microcomputer applications software, as outlined below, there is little overlap between the library's instructional offerings and those of Cornell Computer Services. This is first because we have consistently maintained our focus on the use of microcomputers as tools for the access, retrieval, and control of information. We also consult frequently with CCS, so that both organizations are aware of the plans of the other. CCS tends to concentrate on the use of microcomputers for the creation of information by the user (word processing, for example) and the numerical analysis of information (statistical software) in its workshop program. It also offers discussions of how to choose a microcomputer system for purchase and technical sections in such areas as microcomputer architecture and assembly language routines, operating system behavior, and computer communications.

On any university campus where a library proposes the creation of a new program of computer instruction, an examination of the activities of the academic computing center and conversations with their staff about future plans are certainly important first steps. With the overwhelming demand for computer instruction and support in the university today, it would be difficult to identify an organization less eager to protect its own "turf" than Cornell Computer Services. CCS is pleased to have the cooperation of the libraries in providing instruction in certain facets of the use of microcomputers. This situation probably prevails now at many universities. The danger is not so much that the library's offer to help will be rejected, but that the library may lose sight of its own special goals as it begins to offer computer instruction.

COMPONENTS OF THE CLASSROOM INSTRUCTIONAL PROGRAM

As indicated above, our library teaches computer-related workshops because we believe that online systems and microcomputers are of enormous significance to the future of information retrieval and control. We currently conduct workshops in three principal areas--online database searching, bibliographic file management, and "generic" applications software. The first two of these activities stem directly from the library's concern with the use of computerized information systems. We teach applications software for reasons that might better be described as political, but we do foresee developments that will link standard applications packages such as spreadsheets and database managers to the sorts of research and scholarly information sources that directly concern the library.

The library offers workshops of several types in each of its three areas of computer instruction. First, we teach instructional sessions that constitute a component of regular courses in our two client colleges. In these cases we work closely with the college faculty to insure that our instruction is well integrated with the overall coverage and sequence of the course. Second, we offer "open workshops" which are available to the entire Cornell community. People interested in these sessions may sign up in person or by telephone. Third, the library also participates, in conjunction with Cornell Computer Services, in programs of computer instruction provided twice a year to Cornell faculty through the sponsorship of the Dean of the Faculty's office. This faculty program has run now for three years, with increasing emphasis on microcomputing. Its intent is to provide instructional opportunities to faculty members who wish to use a microcomputer or who feel they need a better understanding of computing. These sessions are conducted during the intersession periods between academic semesters, when faculty members are most likely to be free from their teaching responsibilities. Finally, in addition to these regular programs, library instructors often make presentations on online searching and information technology to campus and external groups. The Online Classroom, in particular, gives us a facility where we can support these presentations with on-screen demonstrations of functioning computer systems.

The remainder of this section of Chapter 8 will outline the three areas of computer instruction. In addition, we will touch on the teaching of subject-specific software, data files, and expert systems--fields where we expect to be active in the future. Chapters 9 through 12 treat the current components of the library's instructional program in detail. Chapter 13 focuses on a somewhat different area--microcomputer support for the library's own staff.

Teaching Online Searching

The library has offered instruction in end-user database searching since summer 1983. We initially targeted classes in the College of Human Ecology, and now also teach within courses of the College of Agriculture and in our open workshop format. This is currently the largest component of the library's instructional program. During the 1985-86 academic year, for example, we taught 51 classes and a total of 872 students. We also put on three workshops for faculty.

In addition to classroom instruction and demonstrations, the library provides reference-desk consultation in constructing search strategies and trained coaches to assist novice database searchers. See Chapters 9 and 10 for details on these programs. The library continues to offer intermediated searching as a reference service, relatively independently of the end-user program.

Teaching Bibliographic File Management

The library began to offer instruction in the use of bibliographic file management software in June 1984 in a workshop for Cornell faculty. Bibliographic file managers, now available for microcomputers, allow faculty members and researchers to automate control of their reprint files. The library offers the current version of this workshop in faculty sessions and as an open workshop. We also systematically evaluate new examples of this genre of software as they appear on the market and consult with faculty members who want to automate their citation-management systems. Details on our activities with reprint file managers appear in Chapter 11.

Teaching Generic Applications Software

When the library first sought funding for its Microcomputer Center, we offered to assist our colleges in improving overall student and faculty "computer literacy." One general service we provide in this vein is to make our computer-equipped classrooms available to faculty members who need these facilities for group instruction. The library also offers workshops in what we call "generic" applications software--at present, word-processing, spreadsheet, and database management packages. As is true of our workshops in online searching, we offer these sessions both as components of college courses, where faculty members desire the library's assistance, and as open workshops. The high demand for this sort of instruction at Cornell quickly established this component of computer instruction as a going enterprise. During the Microcomputer Center's first year of operation, the library taught 63 workshops in applications software, involving 1,150 faculty, students, and staff.

Generic applications software is in some sense the orphan of our instructional program. The staff of the Information Technology Section has done most of the teaching, with only occasional assistance from other library professionals. The program grew out of the library's response to a particular instructional need perceived by college administration, rather than from the library's own information-related goals. Still, this is certainly an area in which a library can move quickly to establish its credibility in the computing arena. It is also true, as more data sets become available for use with microcomputers, that certain popular spreadsheets, database managers, and statistical software packages are becoming standard mechanisms of access to information that resides in the library's collections. This tendency may cause us to bring the workshops in applications software--or some new version of them--more fully within the fold of information instruction.

The library's workshops in applications software are discussed in Chapter 12.

Teaching Subject-Specific Software, Data Files, and Expert Systems

In addition to the three major instructional components just outlined, it may be worthwhile to note areas the library feels are appropriate for future instructional efforts. As noted in Chapter 3, the library is beginning to collect subject applications related to agriculture, nutrition, the life sciences, biotechnology, and other fields within our collection scope. There is some possibility that we would offer limited instruction in the more popular of these packages, as a service to the faculty.

An important part of traditional bibliographic instruction has been to teach the library patron to competently use printed sources of information. By extension, we feel it is part of our mission to teach users to access and manipulate data stored in machine-readable formats. We are beginning, for example, to collect files of data stored on floppy diskette. As noted in the previous section, the user must typically learn an applications software package in order to control these data, and must go through procedures that can grow complex in order to read the raw data into the applications package. This function of applications software can present a library with the justification to teach "standard" packages such as Lotus and dBase as tools of information access. The library may also wish to address the content of the data files themselves.

A recent development in the data files area is the rapid emergence of compact disk as a storage medium. The space savings associated with compact disk, and the potential of search-and-retrieval software running on a microcomputer, is such that this may become the medium of choice for many standard indexes and reference works in the next several years. If this proves the case, even libraries that do not install microcomputer centers will be faced with the need to teach patrons how to operate compact-disk search-and-retrieval systems. As libraries have already learned with online systems, vendors may claim that their search systems are simple and self-explanatory, but patrons will surely require considerable instruction and support if they are to effectively employ the new technology.

In Chapter 3 we stated that the library accorded a high priority to the collection of microcomputer-based expert systems because these packages represent, ultimately, another way of organizing and accessing information. An expert system supports both a "knowledge base" and a set of rules that allow the user to draw forth from the database those pieces of information that are appropriate to a particular set of circumstances. Because of this close and innovative link to information, the library is willing to teach as well as to collect this category of microcomputer software.

AUDIENCES AND NEEDS

The Patrons of Mann Library

As the largest science library at Cornell, and as a library with the mission of supporting research, instruction, and Cooperative Extension activities within two colleges and two academic divisions that conduct extremely diverse programs, Mann Library patrons potentially range from undergraduates in a design course, to research faculty members working in biotechnology, to county extension agents. In structuring our instructional program in information retrieval and control, and in the use of microcomputers and applications software, we have tried to retain a focus on what we feel are the true library uses of microcomputers, while providing a scope sufficient to satisfy the needs of these varied clientele.

In the broadest sense, the library has six distinct audiences: undergraduates, graduate students, faculty, staff, administration, and external organizations. Different approaches are required to reach each of these groups effectively.

Undergraduates

As was mentioned in the Introduction, the most dramatic increase in student computing in the past three to five years has taken place not within the curriculum of the Computer Science Department but within the courses of other departments and completely outside the formal curriculum. Undergraduates who have never taken a computer course are ever more aware that knowledge of microcomputers can help them with their academic work and make them more attractive to employers. There is an apparently endless demand for workshops in the use of microcomputers and software. In our experience, most undergraduate students are better informed about standard applications such as word processing and file management than they are about the use of the microcomputer in information retrieval.

As stressed above, our library has felt for several years that systematic instruction in the identification, retrieval, and control of information--by both traditional and automated means--should be part of the undergraduate curriculum. A large proportion of students who participate in our end-user searching program are undergraduates.

Of the college-funded microcomputer centers described in Chapter 1, two are used primarily by college courses that teach computing throughout the academic semester. As indicated in Chapter 2, we felt it important that our Microcomputer Center be available not only for library instructional programs but also to faculty members who wish to develop a component of work based on the microcomputer for inclusion in a course that has not traditionally used computing, in order to encourage the spread of computer training within the colleges.

The use of microcomputers increased rapidly in the curricula of the Colleges of Agriculture and Human Ecology between 1983 and 1985. Students in economics courses, for instance, are now performing quantitative analysis with spreadsheets, having learned to use the software in laboratory sessions early in the semester. Faculty in journalism and communications arts teach students word processing at the beginning of the semester and then insist that the students use a microcomputer to complete assignments. Courses in many academic departments now require students to learn particular applications packages as part of the semester's work. The staff of the Information Technology Section supports this type of computer instruction with the workshops in the use of applications software and with the maintenance of our collection of course-reserve software.

Graduate Students

Graduate students, who are older, who are nearer long-term career choices, and who often feel themselves further removed from the "computer generation" than do undergraduates, are particularly eager to improve their understanding of microcomputers. At least half the attendees in our "open" workshops are graduate students, though undergraduates outnumber graduate students in our colleges by more than three to one. Foreign graduate students are among the most concerned to catch up with the new technology. We taught one workshop in the use of spreadsheets during spring 1985 in which less than half the participants were native speakers of English. Some were sitting in front of a keyboard for the first time.

The needs of graduate students for information retrieval tend to be more specialized and well focused than those of undergraduates. Graduate students seem to have more interest in understanding the scope and limitations of databases and are generally more independent in developing their search strategies. Unlike most undergraduates, they are interested in author searching. Graduate students often own a microcomputer or have access to a machine in an office or laboratory and may be interested in acquiring their own system passwords. We are considering adding an "advanced techniques" workshop to our present offerings in online searching to meet the needs of these increasingly sophisticated users.

Faculty

The interests of the faculty, and consequently their requirements in computing, are specialized and sophisticated. Many faculty members, particularly in the sciences and social sciences, have used mainframe computing for years in their research and are converting to microcomputers as the capabilities of the technology grow to meet their needs. Some use microprocessor-based equipment for data collection in the laboratory and are beginning to explore the potential of microcomputers for data management and analysis, as well as for standard "office automation" applications. Other faculty members who have not used computing in their work before have simply decided that they must make a start.

The library has defined more carefully the spectrum of instruction that we offer to the faculty than we have with our student workshops. Although we have offered a word-processing workshop to the faculty, this was a target of opportunity and will probably be phased out over time. We concentrate in faculty workshops on database searching and managing reprint files with a microcomputer. These areas, we feel, fall closest to the library's expertise and are intimately connected to information access and retrieval. Our understanding with Cornell Computer Services specifies that these are the computer applications in which we specialize, and in which we are willing to offer consulting services to faculty members.

Staff

A microcomputer center in an academic library presents an excellent opportunity to bring systematic computer instruction to library staff. Our Microcomputer Center offered almost 25 workshops for Cornell library staff in the 20 months after the facility opened. These efforts are described in greater detail in Chapter 12.

Administration

The administrations of the colleges and divisions that support Mann Library are a vital audience. In order to gain budgetary support for new library programs, we must convince the deans and directors that library information services matter. On several occasions, we have used our computer-equipped classrooms to illustrate the power of the new information retrieval technologies to administrators. An actual demonstration of a database search is much more convincing than an abstract presentation about the "future" of computerized information retrieval. It is one responsibility of the library to keep administrators aware of what can be accomplished with current technology.

External Groups

In the last 18 months, the library has entertained many audiences from outside the immediate Cornell community. These include groups of Cooperative Extension agents, Cornell alumni, the advisory councils of our sponsoring colleges, visitors from abroad, and visitors from other libraries. The interests and needs of these groups vary of course, but the presence of the Microcomputer Center in the library allows us to make convincing presentations of automated information technology. Demonstrations of database searching have been well received. Cooperative Extension agents, who work throughout New York State, are interested in learning about the capabilities of microcomputers for interoffice communications and information dissemination. Librarians in developing countries are extremely interested in the potential of inexpensive microcomputers for the support of automated library functions.

CONSULTATIVE SERVICES

Instruction and Consultation

One reason to offer group instruction in information access and control is simple efficiency--what you manage to convey to a class you may possibly avoid having to communicate to a succession of individuals at the reference desk. Though this may sound logical, it does not always apply to the teaching of automated systems and microcomputer software. In actuality, the more a library teaches its patrons in this area, the higher their expectations and the more sophisticated the range of questions with which they will confront you. At the very best, an active program of instruction in computerized information systems must be supported by a systematic approach to consultation with those who try to put to use the skills they have learned in the workshops.

Each of the major components of our instructional program generates a body of patrons with their own particular consulting needs. The sections that follow describe these groups and how we try to assist them.

Consulting Audiences I–End-User Searching

Faculty members and students are obtaining their own passwords and accounts in order to search databases from their homes, offices, or laboratories. While the library may have chosen a particular end-user system for its instructional program, librarians need to be familiar with a range of commercial systems in order to advise patrons on the best choice for their needs. Vendors are usually willing to send multiple copies of their brochures for librarians to hand out to interested patrons. In addition, the library may want to develop a chart comparing search services or a bibliography listing articles which describe the services.

Patrons may ask librarians or technical staff members to consult on equipment needs and configuration for database searching. We are willing to visit offices and laboratories to assist with equipment configuration, and to try a sample search using the library account before a faculty member acquires his or her password. We also advise on the acquisition of database manuals and thesauri. Once a patron begins to search outside the library, we still are interested in maintaining a consultative role. We continue to advise on such concerns as search strategy development, choice of database, and new products on the market.

Consulting Audiences II–
Bibliographic File Management

The principal audiences for our workshops in bibliographic file management software are researchers and faculty members, most of whom already support manual reprint files. Workshop participants who find the classroom session convincing are thereby in a position to begin developing an automated system for the control of their reprint files, generating a good deal of demand for consulting services. Faculty members are interested in having our librarians work with them to identify a software package appropriate to their needs, and then often want assistance in getting started. Our support role can involve anything from software configuration, to database indexing design, to instruction in how a microcomputer keyboard works. When the citation file is developed from a downloaded computer search, the librarian is often asked to assist with the reformatting of the file to meet the requirements of the bibliographic management package. This type of individual assistance requires a broad set of skills, and can be very time consuming. We have set up guidelines that specify how far the library will carry consultation and other services in this area before we charge the patron.

Consulting Audiences III–
"Generic" Applications Software

The library's workshops in standard applications software packages encourage those library patrons who use the Microcomputer Center's machines and software collection--mostly undergraduates and graduate students--to depend on the computer to help them complete their academic work. The burden of the consulting demand that results falls on the student employees in the Microcomputer Center. See Chapter 7 for information on how we train and prepare our student assistants to cope with patron questions.

SUMMARY

1. Information is becoming the vital resource in the "postindustrial" economy, while microcomputer technology is providing new ways to access and manage information in the university and the corporation. These trends in information and computing offer academic libraries the opportunity to extend their traditional role of teaching patrons to locate and organize scholarly information.

2. Although libraries must continue to offer "bibliographic instruction" in the use of printed sources, a library instruction program should present a broad set of offerings designed to improve the "information literacy" of patrons. We treat both bibliographic and nonbibliographic information in our instructional program and teach patrons to locate that information by both manual and automated means.

3. A library that does not offer credit-bearing courses may wish to work with the faculty to integrate its workshops into courses. One broad goal appropriate to a library instructional program is to see instruction in "information literacy" gain official standing within the university's curricula, so that all students receive training in the use of information resources before they graduate.

4. Before embarking on a program of computer-based instruction, a library should coordinate its efforts with those of the campus computing center. For example, our workshops in information access and control with a microcomputer complement the offerings of Cornell Computer Services. In coordinating its instructional program with that of the campus computing agency, the library should insure that it retains its focus on the transfer and organization of information.

5. Workshops in online database searching, bibliographic file management, and applications software packages are among the possibilities for a library's instructional program. Although our sessions in applications software derive from a commitment to the support of computer literacy that the library made when the Microcomputer Center was funded, certain applications packages are coming into use as tools of information access. In the future, the library may add workshops in subject-specific software, data files (including compact-disk based search-and-retrieval systems), and expert

systems. These areas are all related to the use of the microcomputer to access and control scholarly information.

6. Possible models for workshops include course-integrated sessions undertaken in cooperation with the faculty, "open" workshops available to the entire campus community, special training sessions for faculty participants, presentations to external groups, and training workshops for library staff.

7. Teaching personnel should adjust the contents of information literacy workshops to meet the needs of particular audiences. We alter the content and approach of our workshops according to the requirements of at least six groups: undergraduates, graduate students, faculty, staff, administration, and external organizations.

8. An instructional program in the use of microcomputer technology to access, retrieve, and control information generates a heavy load of consulting work. Each workshop program will give rise to a distinct consulting audience. We have developed rational mechanisms for handling this burden by coordinating our consulting efforts with Cornell Computer Services and by defining when the library will charge for its consultative services.

Chapter 9

Teaching Users to Search External Databases: Instruction

Joan Lippincott, Linda Stewart, and Bill Coons

END-USER INSTRUCTION ARRIVES

In the mid-1980s, end-user instruction was suddenly the talk of the library profession. The term "end-user searching" denotes that the patrons who will actually use the end product--information, whether bibliographic or otherwise, retrieved from an online database--search the system themselves, rather than having an "intermediary"--a librarian or information professional-- conduct the search. Numerous conferences and workshops chose end-user searching as their theme and many academic and special libraries made plans to launch programs that would allow patrons to search online databases. From 1983 to 1984, Janke noted an increase from six to 31 libraries that either planned or were currently implementing end-user searching.[1]

While this concept of end-user searching has come to the fore recently, librarians have actually experimented with teaching students, faculty members, researchers, and professionals to perform their own database searches for at least ten years. Nevertheless, the appearance of the BRS menu-driven After Dark Service, DIALOG's simplified command-driven system Knowledge Index, and Information Access's menu-driven Search Helper marked the beginning of a new era of searching. No longer did users of online systems have to learn a command language or spend large sums of money in order to search. The new systems permitted novices to undertake searches at low cost, thus making it reasonable for users to perform their own searches without depending on a professional.

In establishing end-user searching, a library must decide whether its program will be an adjunct of reference service, where users consult the database without formal preparation knowing that brief interaction with a professional is available, or whether the program will emphasize instruction. Chapters 9 and 10 will discuss the establishment of end-user programs with an instructional focus.

THE RATIONALE FOR TEACHING
END-USERS

While teaching students and faculty to perform their own database searches is less controversial than it once was, a profession-wide commitment to the instruction of end-users is still lacking in the library world. Some professionals think of end-user instruction as a gimmick or an add-on service. We feel it should become an integral part of an academic library's service program. As stated in Chapter 8, in today's information society the mission of the library to assist its users in locating and retrieving information should apply regardless of the format of the source. From the perspective of the patron, the skills required to search databases are increasingly important to competent performance in universities and the professional world. End-user instruction thus presents an opportunity for an academic library to play an important part in the education of its patrons.

End-user instruction falls naturally to the library for three reasons: (1) information seekers increasingly need access to online databases with which librarians are familiar, (2) librarians are uniquely qualified to teach people to use search-and-retrieval interfaces, and (3) computerized systems are strongly entrenched as part of the information picture. Librarians are well aware of the advantages of using online databases rather than their print equivalents in many situations. While patrons may not be as sophisticated in database searching as librarians, their information needs are frequently modest. They may not require comprehensive results that demand advanced searching skills. Users may also wish to conduct searches that librarians consider too simple for online retrieval. If the user is making an informed decision, however, the librarian should respect this judgment. Many users would rather conduct a computer search and have their references printed out quickly and conveniently than search manually through a number of years of a printed reference tool and copy out relevant citations. This is a reasonable choice. In many cases, of course, people's information needs clearly call for an online search, by anyone's standards. Here the question is only who should search--librarian or patron--and again, why should the library not allow the patron to make an informed choice?

In any case, there is a sizable population, according to Janke's studies and our own in-house survey, who would prefer to conduct searches themselves, with a librarian present to assist, rather than have a librarian conduct searches for them. In teaching students to search, librarians thus meet patron expectations, as well as equip patrons with skills that will be valuable in their professional lives.

Many librarians in academic environments already have expertise in online retrieval and also teach traditional library skills to their constituents. If academic public services librarians are not yet adept at online information retrieval, they should update their skills as quickly as possible. As experts in information retrieval, as interpreters of tools that employ controlled vocabularies, and as specialists in the organization and indexing of information, librarians are uniquely qualified to teach database searching.

Librarians must promote themselves and their skills and establish themselves within their institutions as authorities on online information sources and retrieval techniques. In some cases, faculty members have assumed responsibility for instructing their students to search and have kept the program disassociated from the library. We believe that the library should be the focal point for instruction in finding, retrieving, and controlling information in its various forms. With our perspective on the universe of information, our knowledge of the range of commercial systems, and our skills in formulating search strategies, it is librarians who can best teach users to become informed consumers of online information systems.

Online retrieval systems marketed for the end-user are a present and probably permanent reality. Researchers, students, and computer buffs learn about them from colleagues, from articles and advertisements in computer magazines, and from promotional materials. Though librarians are the logical interpreters and advisors for these systems, vendors now do not generally associate their systems with libraries. Some librarians hurt their professional image by refusing to add instruction and consultation in online searching to their services. With some students now being taught to search in secondary and even elementary schools, there will be an ever-increasing demand for instruction in online retrieval. Librarians must stay a step ahead of their users to meet the challenge of coping with information today.

THE GOALS AND OBJECTIVES OF INSTRUCTION

In designing instructional programs, we distinguish between "goals" and "objectives." Typically, goals represent the larger outcomes that we hope to achieve through our instructional activities--in the case of end-user searching, the set of concepts and skills that we want participants to take away from our classroom workshops and coached search sessions. "Objectives" are narrower in scope, and serve, in effect, as milestones that indicate to us whether we are making measurable progress toward the achievement of our goals.

A library can approach the establishment of goals by determining the level of expertise it seeks to foster in its patrons. The most ambitious goal would be to bring the patron to the level of the professional search analyst. Few programs (except those designed to train search analysts) attempt so much. In many programs, the intention is that end-users will perform their own "simple" searches and refer other searches to an intermediary. Simple searches are defined variously as:

> Searches that are exploratory, as opposed to those that are comprehensive.
> Searches that include few basic concepts.
> Searches that do not require advanced features such as paragraph qualification or truncated concept codes.

Some programs have end-users work within a specific framework--with presearch counseling (Janke, 1985)[2], with printed search aids (Wharton, 1985)[3], or with the assistance of a trained coach at the first search (Mann Library). A library may wish to spend some time considering these options when it establishes the goals of a training program in online searching.

Our library teaches online searching as part of a broader educational goal. Our original rationale was that, just as students use printed reference materials on their own, they should have the option of using online reference sources themselves. We also see the program as contributing to the computer literacy and "information literacy" of our student clientele. We would like to provide students with a bank of skills and concepts applicable to the searching of current-generation online databases which they can transfer to other systems that they will encounter later in their careers. We try to make this experience so positive that our students will approach online information retrieval with enthusiasm and confidence.

At Mann Library the formal goals for our end-user searching program are:

1. To familiarize participants with the availability of online retrieval systems, and with the advantages and disadvantages of conducting their own database searches.

2. To provide participants with an adequate background to decide which online system will best meet their needs.

3. To teach participants the procedures necessary to perform their own searches on one particular system.

4. To provide participants with a set of concepts that will enable them to adapt easily to diverse online systems.

Given the goal of transferability, we are not anxious that the individual student become an expert in the particular online system that we currently employ. We would, however, like students to approve of their search results. To this aim, we have established for our program of instruction in end-user searching the following objectives, which serve to indicate to us that our goals have been accomplished:

1. *Participants can define a bibliographic database, can give an example of a database, and describe the subject coverage of what is being searched on the BRS After Dark system.*
[We want students to be aware that online databases are often commercially produced, are unconnected with Cornell's library holdings or mainframe computers, and can be accessed by the general public.]
2. *Given a list and a brief description of available databases, participants can choose one or more databases appropriate to their topic.*
[Students should understand that databases are usually organized around a theme--that is, a database will include materials relating to a particular subject area, or of a specific format.]
3. *Given an appropriate thesaurus, participants can choose terms relevant to their topic and can add free text words as needed.*
[Most systems retrieve materials based on exact or near matches to submitted terms. Students need to anticipate all terms which an author or indexer may have used to describe an item.]
4. *Participants can construct logical search strategies for their topics by identifying concepts and using Boolean operators to link terms and manipulate sets.*
[This involves defining one's topic in such a way that the request can be understood by an online system.]
5. *Participants can respond to screen prompts to input their search strategies on a terminal or microcomputer and execute the steps needed to print citations.*
[Since search protocols are often forgotten if they are not reinforced by hands-on experience, an actual search is part of the program.]
6. *Participants can list the advantages and limitations of computer searching as compared to manual searching and can recognize conditions when a computer search is likely to be more effective than a manual search.*
[We want students to understand the potential of online searching, yet not consider it a panacea for all information needs.]

7. *Participants can recognize situations in which their own searching should be supplemented by searching performed by a professional.*
[Students need to realize that they have received only a basic level of training. The fact that a search does not produce useful results does not mean that nothing has been written on the topic in question. Students should not be discouraged when a search is fruitless--they should seek assistance.]

COMPONENTS OF THE END-USER PROGRAM

The components of the library's program of instruction in the searching of databases--that is, the format of the learning experiences we provide and the amount of time spent on each--derive from our educational goals. We currently use the BRS After Dark system in our training program, for reasons that will be treated in the next chapter. Although BRS After Dark is a simplified search system, designed for inexperienced searchers, we concluded that students could benefit from staff assistance during three processes: initial introduction to the system, formulation of search strategy for individual topics and databases, and actual execution of a search.

The first component in our program is a one to one-and-a-half hour classroom presentation including a discussion of the basics of the online system and a demonstration search. Where the entire class will use one database, we treat this database in detail. We originally held these group sessions in the Microcomputer Center classroom. However, as only the instructor needs to use a microcomputer, we have now moved these workshops to the Online Classroom.

The second component in the sequence is a reference interview with a professional online searcher. The library requires that the student complete this interview before performing a search for the first time. Students fill out a worksheet that leads them to select a database and design a search strategy for a topic of their own choosing, usually related to a required research paper. The searcher ascertains that students have expressed their search strategies using proper Boolean logic and acquaints them with any thesauri available for the databases they have chosen. At the end of the interview, the searcher signs the worksheet to indicate that the student has completed the second component of the training program.

Component three is the actual search. When students perform their searches as part of credit courses, academic departments fund the first half-hour to hour of searching. This subsidy serves to motivate students to start searching while the details remain fresh in their minds. Two students usually search at adjacent microcomputers, with one library staff member, referred to as a "coach," present to provide assistance. These coaches log students onto the system, insure the proper performance of the microcomputer and printer, collect any fees due, and consult with the searchers during their online sessions. The coaches remind students of search commands and help them broaden, narrow, or refine their searches. Originally, only reference librarians served as coaches; now the library also uses specially trained teaching assistants and student assistants from the staff of the Microcomputer Center.

We find all three parts of this program essential. Many students, particularly undergraduates, are unfamiliar with Boolean logic and controlled vocabulary prior to the workshop. Simply presenting information in a classroom is sufficient for some participants; others will appear at the reference desk for their interview without a clear understanding of how to formulate a search strategy. Some students encounter difficulty with such "traditional" operations as defining their topics. The opportunity for individualized assistance before students go online is thus crucial.

Even when students have completed the interview and understand their search strategy, they need help in interacting with an online system. Despite media claims of widespread computer use in high schools, many of our student clients have never used a computer before. The library coaches provide simple reassurance, proofreading skills, and, most importantly, advice on how to proceed when the system produces an unexpected result.

Basically, the three components in our end-user program function as an insurance system. Students who do not understand an important concept at the workshop have two subsequent opportunities to receive assistance--during the interview and during their search. By the end of their first search, most participants thereby succeed in grasping the basic concepts of searching that we try to communicate.

OUTLINE OF CLASS SESSIONS

The content of the class session that is the first component in our end-user program has changed several times. We also adapt the basic material to meet the particular needs of different audiences. Nevertheless, we have retained our primary aim, that users grow able to independently search online information systems in an efficient, consistent, and logical manner. The library also endeavors to keep the instruction basic and the search procedures simple, no matter what the audience. Our present class outline is based upon a familiarity with the literature of end-user searching and upon our actual experiences. The following is a summary of the material we cover in our workshops, though we do not always proceed in the order listed.

1. Explain what an online database is, differentiating between bibliographic, numeric, and full-text files. Place the definition of an online database in context by referring to print equivalents, the overall scope of information and its varying formats, and methods of retrieval. We find it useful to use a printout of one record from a particular database, and then to build a description of the database and how it is searched from the components of that record.

2. Briefly elaborate on the process of gaining access to databases, the types of systems and vendors available, and the costs of online searching. We have found that it is particularly important to emphasize that the databases students will search are unrelated to and remote from Cornell University.

3. Point out the advantages of searching (convenience, speed, and ability to combine different concepts and words), while realistically describing some of the disadvantages and instances where a computer search may not be appropriate. We emphasize that computers are not a cure-all in information access, and that online and print sources complement each other. We also distinguish between instances where end-user searching is appropriate and where mediated searching is indicated. We then describe the range of library search services available to patrons.

4. Emphasize the choices a searcher must make and the consequences those choices have for an online search. These would include choice of a topic, choice of database, choice of subject terms, and choice of keywords. A presentation of the general principles of formulating a systematic search strategy for information is effective here. A searcher's topic should be neither too broad nor too narrow; alternative strategies need to be prepared in advance for use if a search produces too many or too few citations. The searcher must subdivide a topic into discrete facets or concepts. The databases one selects will influence the structure of the search questions, the types and numbers of keywords that one chooses, and the relevance of the citations one retrieves to the topic one has defined. Finally, we stress that the identification and selection of appropriate vocabulary (keywords, descriptors, and synonyms) affects the quality of a search.

We next describe the use of thesauri, controlled vocabulary, and free text. Practical examples involving choice of vocabulary are presented. For example, we explain the need to use sets of synonyms such as "ascorbic acid or vitamin C," "cystic ovary or ovarian cysts," "lucerne or alfalfa or medicagoy sativa," or "yogurt or yoghurt or yogourt or yoghourt."

5. Describe the database access procedures and search commands. Keyboard mechanics are extremely important. Searchers need to know what key or combination of keys will allow them to backspace, shift, print, download, and send the system a carriage return. The appropriate use of the Boolean triumvirate, *AND*, *OR*, and *NOT*, is explained, and special system features such as truncation, proximity searching, paragraph qualification, and command stacking are introduced. Depending on the level of detail of the workshop, we may explore one or more of these features in detail.

6. Reiterate that not everything retrieved in a search will be relevant to the search topic, and that some of the materials identified will not be held in the home library. Sometimes librarians forget to treat document retrieval when they teach online methods of information access. Computer printouts, full of tags and abbreviations, need to be explained so that users can interpret citations well enough to attempt to locate materials in their host libraries. The instructor should stress that online databases are not listings of what is available at a searcher's own institution, and that references identified but not available locally must be obtained from other sources through the interlibrary loan department.

7. Explain the search appointment schedule, the steps necessary for initiating a search, the costs involved, and the methods of payment.

We find that this outline works well in a general introductory workshop. When we want to present advanced searching techniques or to treat topics specific to particular subject areas or particular databases, we modify or enhance the basic offerings. We also find it necessary to modify the content of the workshop depending on the needs of our audience and their level of sophistication. Seminars for undergraduate students are not as thorough or all-encompassing as those for faculty members and graduate students. We have found that much of our demand for instruction comes from faculty members who are teaching undergraduate courses and want to integrate some aspect of computer literacy into their classroom material. They may also want to take advantage of an online system's ability to help students with research for term papers.

As a result of this sort of faculty interest, we perform the majority of our workshops for students in particular classes. Open workshops, as opposed to course-related instruction, make up a smaller but significant portion of our end-user instructional program. The library's end-user workshops for faculty members have been well attended during the intersession programs. Special departmental presentations are also important because they give us the opportunity to reach influential and potentially supportive audiences of faculty.

A variety of instructional aids exists which can help facilitate training and searching. Some, like handouts with search examples and commands, are commonplace, essential, and effective. Others, such as computer assisted instruction programs and written or audiovisual training aids, are used less extensively. Eisenberg has stated that "studies of various instructional approaches [regarding the training of end-users] have found each to be useful in improving performance," although "studies of the effectiveness of any particular training methodology have been generally inconclusive."[4] A developing area with considerable potential in training is that of database subsets accessed with search-and-retrieval software running on a microcomputer (such as ERIC's MICROsearch) or flexible tutorials on diskette. These methods remove the cost constraint of online connect time and allow end-users to practice at their own pace. In our library, nevertheless, we have decided that there is no good substitute for effective demonstrations, convincing, concise lectures, and positive hands-on experience. No matter how much we tell end-users about searching, some of the concepts prove elusive until patrons actually search under the guidance of trained personnel.

EVALUATION

The evaluation of end-user search programs is useful in assessing their value to a library's clientele and in planning changes in the training sequence. Long-range studies, examining the ultimate impact of these programs on the way that people gather and use information, are also greatly needed.

Most institutions sponsoring end-user search programs have conducted some evaluation, even if this has involved only the collection of use statistics. Other factors of interest will depend on program goals but will fall into the general categories of the demographic characteristics of the end-users, their subjective reactions to the search service, and their objective ability to search.

Demographic variables commonly examined include age, sex, status at the institution, purpose of search, previous computer training or experience, time spent online, and number and type of databases searched.

Subjective factors often include the perceived ease of searching, the motivation for further use of the service, and satisfaction with:

1. The number and relevance of references retrieved.
2. The cost and availability of the search service.
3. The quality of the library's training, counseling, and user aids.

Occasionally libraries also venture to solicit suggestions for improving their programs, focusing on areas such as the type of assistance that patrons prefer and acceptable cost ranges.

Instructors working in end-user programs sometimes construct objective measures to examine individual ability to perform an adequate search. Assessments may be made of the user's understanding of:

1. What is being searched.
2. Command structure or menus.
3. Boolean operators.
4. Vocabulary control.

The participant's ability to interact with the hardware and software may be examined, along with the need for outside assistance. Some programs have attempted to analyze the overall adequacy of search results, evaluating them against previously established criteria.[5]

Questionnaires and interviews are common vehicles for evaluation, particularly in treating subjective reactions to the service. Pre- and post-tests evaluate attitudes toward searching and users' understanding of online systems. Some unobtrusive methods can also prove valuable, such as examination of transaction records[6] and standardized observation of users by staff.[7]

Our library has undertaken several small-scale evaluation projects in conjunction with the program in end-user searching. One, a survey of the demographic characteristics and subjective reactions of end-users, was conducted in fall 1984. Our latest project represents a broader attempt to assess the motivation and skill levels of searchers, before and after their online experience. The evaluation instrument is now being pretested.

The 1984 survey, which included graduate students and under-graduates, concluded that users felt that both the introductory workshop and the subsequent reference interview were useful. They found the BRS After Dark system easy to use and were satisfied with the relevancy of their search results.

Fifty-three percent of the respondents conducted online searches only once, while 47 percent did so two or more times. We were particularly interested in the reasons why participants performed only one search, considering this an indirect indication of reactions to the program. The following reasons were cited, with some respondents mentioning more than one:

46.0 percent--I had no further need for information.
11.5 percent--I was dissatisfied with the results.
11.5 percent--It was too expensive.
19.0 percent--I would have had to pay for additional searching.
8.0 percent--I had difficulty scheduling another appointment.

It appears that dissatisfaction with results was not a major reason for not searching further; an absence of a need to search again and the cost of the service were more frequently cited. The program seems to have converted most participants to online searching; 89 percent think they will use the service again.

For our latest evaluation project, we are examining the general experience of participants in our instructional program in database searching. As explained in the section on goals and objectives, we try to make students aware of the potential of online searching, to increase their confidence in their ability to perform their own searches, and to provide them with a set of transferable skills which they can apply to other computer systems, such as an online catalog. The evaluation instrument consists of a questionnaire to be administered both before search training and after performance of at least one online search.

We examine attitude change with a series of statements with which the student may strongly disagree, disagree, agree, or strongly agree. Statements measure the student's recognition of the material benefits of searching, assurance that searching skills can be learned, and recognition that the outcome of the training in online searching represents a desirable personal accomplishment.

We test the skill level of participants through a series of multiple-choice questions. Students must show an understanding of what is meant by a commercial online database--by distinguishing it from an online catalog, for instance. Students are asked which of several search statements could have retrieved a sample citation. Statements also test for an understanding of the need for an exact match between search terms and terms contained in the reference, the use of the operators *AND* and *OR*, and proper grouping of terms. Finally, respondents are asked to indicate acceptable ways to broaden and narrow sample search statements. We hope that this evaluation instrument will prove an accurate indicator of both attitude change and retention of basic skills.

SUMMARY

1. The introduction of "user-friendly" search systems by the major vendors of online systems has helped make database searching practical for end-users. As online systems are now an established and important part of the universe of scholarly information, librarians should take the opportunity to offer instruction in online search-and-retrieval. Library professionals are

uniquely qualified to teach database searching because of their experience in information retrieval, the use of controlled vocabularies, and the organization and indexing of information.

2. Training in online information retrieval is an important component of an overall program in "information literacy" which seeks to make the student as competent and independent as possible in the location and use of information. The library program should seek to provide students with a set of transferable skills that will assist them in mastering any information-access system they may encounter. At the same time, an end-user training program should give workshop participants actual exposure to at least one search system and instill confidence that they can search successfully.

3. Under our formulation, training in end-user searching consists of three components--a lecture and on-screen demonstration of search procedures, a reference interview, and a hands-on search experience. A library coach is present when participants first search. This three-part sequence works to insure that all students understand the basic principles of searching when they have completed the program.

4. A library will wish to vary the content of its workshops in data-base searching to meet the needs of particular audiences, but it helps to work from a comprehensive outline. Given the computing background of many of the students who attend our sessions, we find it important to stress that the online databases under discussion do not reside on the university computers.

5. Evaluation is an important part of a program of training in database searching. We have conducted several limited evaluation projects in connection with our library's end-user program. Our most recent instrument is designed to help us better understand the background that library patrons bring to the training sessions and their perceptions of online information access. Our results thus far suggest that the majority of our clientele like the idea of conducting their own database searches.

Notes

1. Richard V. Janke, "Online After Six: End User Searching Comes of Age," *Online* 15-29 (Nov. 1984).

2. Ibid.

3. "Do-It-Yourself Information Retrieval at the Wharton School," *BRS Bulletin* 9(11): 11 (Dec. 1985).

4. M. Eisenberg, *The Direct Use of Online Bibliographic Information Systems by Untrained End-Users: A Review of Research*, ED 238 440 (Syracuse: ERIC, 1983).

5. See Charles T. Meadow, Thomas Hewett, and Elizabeth S. Aversa, "A Computer Intermediary for Interactive Database Searching. II. Evaluation," *Journal of the American Society for Information Science* 33(6): 357-64 (Nov. 1982). Also Nicholas Caruso and Elaine Caruso, "TRAINER--A Computer Tutorial for End-Users of Database Services: Context, Content, and Results of Use," *Information Services and Use* 3: 191-98 (1983); Nancy Fjallbrant, Elisabeth Kihlen, and Margareta Malmgren, "End-User Training in the Use of a Small Swedish Database," *College and Research Libraries* 44(2): 161-67 (Mar. 1983).

6. Elaine Trzebiatowski, "End User Study on BRS/After Dark," *RQ* : 446-50 (Summer 1984); Nancy Fjallbrant et al., op. cit.

7. Maureen Corcoran, Richard Copeland, and Dennis Clayton, "Subject Specialists Searching Chemical Abstracts on SDC," *Proceedings of the 43rd ASIS Annual Meeting* 17: 345-47 (1980); James E. Crooks, "End User Searching at the University of Michigan Library," *Proceedings of the National Online Meeting*, 1985 : 99-112 (1985); Nancy Fjallbrant et al., op. cit.

Chapter 10

Teaching Users to Search External Databases: Program Administration

Joan Lippincott, Linda Stewart, and Bill Coons

The development of any new library program, particularly one in an evolving field such as teaching users to complete their own online searches, requires thoughtful and thorough planning. The intent of this chapter is to review some of the administrative concerns a library must address as it develops an end-user search program.

MARKETING THE END-USER INSTRUCTION PROGRAM

Selecting the right target audience is a key first step in establishing an effective and continuing end-user searching program. Large libraries typically identify discrete groups of clientele to participate in a pilot program. Small libraries, on the other hand, may consider their entire user population to be their target audience. The target group will become trendsetters in the institution if the program is successful. They can provide the library's program with excellent publicity. Criteria to consider in the selection of target audiences include:

1. The group's need for information retrieved online.
2. Availability of appropriate databases.
3. Limitations of printed sources in the area of interest of the group.
4. Level of sophistication of the group in the use of computers and information.
5. Funding sources.
6. Campus political factors.

As with most types of library instruction, success in an end-user searching program depends on whether the users truly have an immediate need for the kinds of information they will retrieve online. Undergraduates with term paper assignments, graduate students beginning research, and actively publishing faculty members, for instance, all have a need to identify citations to journal literature in their subject fields. Nevertheless, if appropriate databases are not available, their needs may not be satisfied by online searching. This remains particularly true in the humanities.

If, on the other hand, the library can identify users frustrated by the limitations of the print tools in their fields, and appropriate sources are available online, these patrons may serve as an excellent target group. The nature and extent of the information needs of a user group may also be an important factor in selecting a target audience. If the skills that the library teaches are to be useful for more than one semester, groups with continuing needs are logical targets. In some instances, a program will be successful only if the costs of searching are partially or fully subsidized. If the library is unable to carry this financial burden alone, choosing a target audience that has funds to contribute can give an important boost to a fledgling program.

Finally, political factors can be important in determining a target audience. For example, a department with high visibility and prestige can lend credibility to the new program and assist in spreading the word to others. Influential faculty or departments can assist in securing funds for the program.

At Cornell, our initial target audience was the College of Human Ecology. Having read that the college had funds for a computer literacy program, we approached the project coordinator and suggested that information literacy would be a useful component of their program. We knew that databases were available in the social science fields served by the college and that users often expressed frustration with the limitations of retrieving information from the printed tools. The college response was enthusiastic. We began the program with classes in which students had a demonstrated need to compile bibliographic references. Individual faculty members applied to the college for funds to fully subsidize students' searches. As a result of this choice of a target audience, satisfied faculty members and students spread the word about our search program and helped us reach new groups.

The faculty was our second target audience. We feel it is important that faculty members understand the new end-user searching systems so that they can search for themselves or can arrange for their students to learn to search. Our library has an active research faculty in the sciences and social sciences, who have regular need for bibliographic searches. In addition, many of our faculty members are already aware of the benefits of online information retrieval. As noted in Chapter 8, when we learned of a proposed series of computer literacy workshops for faculty members sponsored by Cornell

Computer Services, we asked to be included in the program. We also requested and received funding for subsidized introductory searches from the Office of the Dean of the Faculty.

In order to gain support for an end-user searching program, the library needs to educate the potential user groups and funding administrators about the usefulness of online information retrieval and the availability of user-friendly systems. To this end, there is no substitute for actual demonstrations of online systems to faculty and administrators. Wherever possible, we have invited departmental chairs to bring their faculty members to the Microcomputer Center during regular departmental meetings for presentations by our professional staff and demonstrations of search systems. Groups of administrators are also often willing to dedicate an hour of meeting time to this activity. On these occasions, providing clear examples of when an online database can be more useful than the print equivalent helps build the case for a program in online searching.

Much of the early promotion of the library's program, if it gets off to a good start, will be by word of mouth. As it becomes feasible to add new groups to the instructional program the library can also employ a number of additional strategies to promote end-user searching. If the university has a computer fair, the library may wish to participate by setting up a booth to demonstrate end-user searching. Vendors will usually supply brochures in quantity and may provide a free password for the day. Demonstrating end-user searching can be an effective adjunct to an open house marking the opening of a microcomputer center or the beginning of a new semester. Articles in campus newspapers, brochures, letters to faculty members, and bulletin board displays can also function well as promotional devices.

THE CHOICE OF AN ONLINE SYSTEM

Once the decision has been made to instruct end-users, a primary concern is what system or systems the library will teach. Choices include the long-established vendors such as BRS and DIALOG, new vendors such as EasyNet, and front-end software packages such as the Sci-Mate Searcher. Among the criteria that the library should weigh before choosing a system are:

1. Equipment required to use the system.
2. Hours of system availability.
3. Cost.
4. Method of payment to vendor.

5. The spectrum of databases available.
6. Whether the system supports command or menu-driven modes.
7. Special features supported.
8. System limitations.
9. Suitability for the target audience.

The remainder of this section will treat these areas of concern.

Equipment Required to Use the System

While the advertising brochures of many of the database systems picture microcomputers, most systems require only a "dumb terminal." If your library or facility already has a terminal and you have limited funds to start an end-user searching program, you may want to choose an online system, such as BRS After Dark or Knowledge Index, where no local processing takes place and a dumb terminal is adequate. The primary advantage of using microcomputers for searching is the ability to download references. If library patrons will want this capability, be careful to purchase microcomputers compatible with those of most of your users. Patrons may wish to use the library's modem-equipped microcomputer and password, download references, and then review and manipulate these citations on their own equipment.

Hours of System Availability

Considerable savings can be realized by searching evenings and weekends; in fact, some systems are only accessible during these off-hours. Choosing a system that is only available evenings and weekends may be suitable for some groups and disastrous with others. Program administrators must relate system availability to staffing needs and the hours the library is open. For example, if you only offer the BRS After Dark system and you routinely close for evenings and weekends during academic intersessions, searching will not be possible during a period that could be convenient for professors and graduate students.

Cost

Depending on the target audience and the funding sources the library has secured, cost of searching may be the most significant factor in the choice of a system or it may carry less weight. Some vendors charge a flat hourly rate, including telecommunications, no matter what database is searched. Such systems simplify the task of passing on charges to the patron. With other systems, charges vary with the database and may include a per-citation fee for references printed. While such systems may offer attractive rates for some databases, they make it difficult to pass on costs to users. Some systems charge by the "search." In such cases, a search is usually defined as a simple combination of terms and the user may have to perform several "searches" to achieve a satisfactory result. Often these systems also limit the number of items that can be printed per search.

Method of Payment to Vendor

The accounting function in most libraries is designed to handle monthly itemized invoices. While some vendors of online services do support this type of invoicing, other vendors require the use of a major credit card, which may violate institutional accounting standards. If an online system is otherwise attractive, the library may find it worthwhile to negotiate an alternative payment mechanism with the vendor.

The Spectrum of Databases Available

For the widest choice of databases, the obvious front-runner is the full DIALOG system. If cost and the need to learn a search language are deterrents, however, a library will need to consider alternatives. The best way to proceed is to define the subject areas of interest to the library's target audience and then to compare these with the offerings of the various vendors.

Command Versus Menu-Driven Modes

If the end-users will be frequent searchers with sophisticated needs, the library may wish to offer a full command system such as BRS, DIALOG, or SDC. On the other hand, if the library anticipates infrequent or irregular use, a menu-driven system, such as BRS After Dark, is probably a better choice. Some services marketed to the end-user, such as Knowledge Index, are not menu-driven but do have simplified command structures.

Special Features Supported

Some user groups may have a particular need for the special features offered by the full systems. An example would be DIALOG's Dialorder document delivery service.

System Limitations

A library should investigate carefully the limitations of the online systems under consideration. Do the databases include all the information available through a full-service system? Are some vital search or limit commands not available? Are patrons constrained to a small number of search terms or documents retrieved? Once the library has identified the limitations of a search system, thought should be given to the impact these will have on search services.

Suitability for the Target Audience

The needs of the target audience are "the bottom line" in choosing a search system. If the library plans to reach disparate groups, perhaps it should offer systems from several vendors or more than one system from a particular vendor.

At our library, we currently offer the BRS After Dark system in our end-user searching program. For our target audience of students and faculty in the life sciences and social sciences, we determined that the most important selection criteria were cost and database availability. The attractive searching rates and ever-increasing list of databases accessible through BRS have, in fact, suited our audience. Another key factor in our choice was the ease of using After Dark menus to perform relatively sophisticated searches. The hours of availability, method of payment to the vendor, and the option of using either dumb terminals or microcomputers also suited our needs. A library with a different audience, or a different set of priorities, however, would likely choose some other vendor.

Communication with Vendors

A successful end-user instruction and search program depends on: (1) the ease of use, comprehensiveness, and dependability of the online system or systems used, (2) the ability of the library to capitalize on these systems and coordinate local access, (3) a receptive group of users, and (4) the cooperation of capable vendors. Most vendors of online systems realize that libraries can do as much for them as they can for us, and welcome cordial and healthy relationships. Vendors who dedicate themselves to the implementation and improvement of end-user searching systems are usually more sensitive to the concerns of their customers than those to whom end-user systems are an ancillary product.

Experienced vendors are receptive to the needs of libraries. They offer suggestions, allocate passwords for demonstrations and instructional purposes, and provide technical support and advice. In return, library sponsorship of end-user searching exposes future professional users to the vendor's system. This exposure serves, in many ways, as a free marketing tool for the vendor. The systems that librarians use and teach today may very well be the same systems end-users will choose for their office or home tomorrow. Strong, open, and frequent communications with responsible vendors can substantially improve the quality of an end-user program.

HARDWARE AND SOFTWARE

Decisions on equipment will depend in part on what the library already owns. If a library intends to order new equipment, one of the most important decisions is whether to use terminals or microcomputers in a searching program. Each has advantages.

"Dumb" terminals, that is, terminals which function only when connected to a remote computer, remain somewhat less expensive than microcomputers. Since no software is needed, additional cost savings are possible. Because terminals have fewer components and logical levels, there are fewer subtleties for the user to master.

Microcomputers are more costly, but definitely provide more capabilities than a terminal. Communications software running on a microcomputer can support the downloading of search results to a diskette, the simplification of search strategy, the entry of an entire strategy before going online, and even accounting functions. The same machine the library uses for searching can perform other tasks as well. Finally, the image from a microcomputer display can be projected on a screen in a classroom, making the microcomputer a more flexible device for group instruction. In our library, group instruction in searching and our coached search sessions both depend exclusively on microcomputers. We have also moved our mediated search services from terminal to microcomputer.

Microcomputers in Online Searching

A microcomputer with a modem performs all the functions of a terminal and, in addition, can run applications software as a stand-alone machine. Microcomputers used for online searching should include at least one disk drive, with a second drive if downloading is desired. The modem can be either "internal" (a board mounted inside the machine) or "external" (usually a small box connected to the serial port of the microcomputer). A telephone cord and telephone wall jack are required, as are power sources for the microcomputer and modem. If references are going to be printed on paper, a printer and computer paper are obviously necessary. For online searching, a dot-matrix printer capable of printing at a rate of 120 characters per second or higher is to be recommended, so that the printer does not substantially slow online communications. Printer speed will become even more critical if 2400-baud communications become the standard. As an alternative approach, a library may decide to download all search results to diskette while online and then to print out these results later. A printer used for end-user searching should permit simple changes of paper and ribbons. Noisy units are to be avoided, as they will interfere with conversation between the end-user and anyone offering counseling.

Software

A microcomputer requires software to run an online search; a terminal cannot be used with software. The first software requirement is an operating system, which provides the environment in which a microcomputer runs commercial applications software. Normally, the operating system software is purchased with the microcomputer hardware. Another necessity is a communications package, which controls the computer-to-computer interaction with the systems operated by the commercial database vendors. In addition, there are many "search assistance" or gateway packages that may enhance an end-user search program. These packages support combinations of the following capabilities:

1. Masking of passwords and log-on procedures, and automated log-on.
2. Menu-driven or simplified searching protocols.
3. Translation from the syntax of a local search language into the syntax of one or more online systems.
4. Submission of search strategies previously typed in offline (uploading).

5. Transferring search results onto diskette or hard disk (downloading).
6. Accounting.
7. Provision of database descriptions.
8. Marking of relevant search results to be printed in a separate report.

Some standard communications packages also provide certain of these functions.

To support our end-user searching program, we have furnished four IBM PCs with internal modems. For communications, we use Hayes Smartcom II communications software. Smartcom II permits automatic log-on, downloading of search results, and uploading of search strategies. Since our program emphasizes the interactive nature of online searching, we do not use the uploading capability. As BRS After Dark is a menu-driven search system, we have not used a search assistance package in our program. Libraries that access other database systems, or have patrons search on the systems of several vendors, would probably find one useful.

Classroom Equipment and Materials

If the instructional component of an end-user search program is to include a demonstration search, some means of projecting a microcomputer's display image will be needed. The two principal options at this time are a video projector and screen or a system of video monitors. A recent development promises to permit the use of an overhead projector for both transparencies and the projection of a microcomputer's screen image. A blackboard remains useful for diagramming search strategies. In a computer facility, a "liquid chalk system" is advisable, as abrasive chalk dust can damage computer equipment.

Should the library wish to provide students with a hands-on experience during the classroom session, a sufficient number of computers will be needed to accommodate participants individually or in small teams, and these computers must have communications connections. This is an expensive proposition at best, though the major vendors have instructional plans where students can search at a lower rate (sometimes using small files) or receive temporary passwords. For some systems, a "canned" tutorial is available that runs locally on a microcomputer. Students can work at their own pace without passwords, telephone lines, or modems, and without incurring online charges. Few of these programs effectively simulate the type of decision making a student will encounter online, however, and motivation may be lower if students are not working on searches actually of interest to them.

Our Online Classroom, described in Chapter 1, provides us with an instructional facility equipped with a microcomputer and modem. We project demonstration searches onto a screen with a video projector. As indicated in Chapter 9, participants do not gain hands-on experience during the class session; this takes place individually by later appointment.

OTHER ADMINISTRATIVE CONCERNS

Staffing

An active instructional program for end-users demands a certain amount of overall coordination. Most libraries will want to vest the responsibility for the program with their Instruction Librarian or Public Services Coordinator. This person can then organize the program, solicit participation by colleagues, and provide the information and leadership necessary to get the library moving.

In addition to the time spent on program administration, the individual responsible for coordinating the program will probably join his or her fellow professionals in teaching the instructional workshops and coaching search sessions. In our library at present, four reference librarians teach workshops and share the task of monitoring and coaching evening search sessions. Distributing the teaching and coaching work prevents any one librarian from becoming overburdened, enriches the content of the classes, and gives more library staff members direct exposure to the program.

The use of student coaches allows us to further distribute the support function in our end-user program. We select these coaches from among the most interested and competent Microcomputer Center student employees and have library professionals train them. In addition, if the professor of a particularly large course wishes to have students complete our program in searching, we often request that a teaching assistant for that class be assigned to the library for training. When the teaching assistant has completed this training, we schedule additional evening and weekend slots for that specific class, to avoid displacing other patrons from the normal blocks of search time because of high demand from the large course. The teaching assistant then coaches students through the search session.

Scheduling

If a library decides to offer end-user instruction to groups, staff members must schedule two kinds of activities--workshops and blocks of time when patrons may perform their own searches. A simple and effective way to begin scheduling is to arrange instructional sessions in advance with the professors who teach selected courses. As the program becomes better known, a need may develop to accommodate students, faculty, and staff who are not associated with a particular course. To meet this demand, the library may wish to introduce general instructional sessions open to all. We initiated our program with several specific classes in the College of Human Ecology and have since expanded its scope to over 25 course-related sessions per year, four intersession workshops for faculty per year, and two open workshops each month.

Factors to consider when scheduling the instructional sessions are the length of each session and the days and times they are to be offered. When instruction is course related, the only possible time is often the regular period for the class, which may be shorter than the library would desire. Workshops scheduled at the library's convenience can run longer--we find 90 minutes ideal for a lecture, demonstration, and discussion--and should be offered at a variety of times--morning, afternoon, and evening. Requiring participants to register in advance for open sessions provides the librarian with an idea of the number of potential attendees, their academic level, and their subject areas of interest. Knowledge of the subject orientation of a group is useful because it helps the instructor select appropriate examples for discussion of databases, choose vocabulary, and structure search demonstrations.

The library needs also to establish times when patrons may actually run their searches. Some institutions, like the University of Pittsburgh's Microcomputer Searching Laboratory, offer their facilities almost constantly but to date provide little assistance; others, including Mann Library, limit end-user searching to selected days and times.

With limited hours and high demand, search sessions can be hectic. We avoid confusion, queues, and hard feelings by using an appointment system. To assure themselves a search, patrons must sign up in advance. Walk-ins are accepted only if the individual is prepared and a time slot is open. We run two searches simultaneously on adjacent machines, with patrons registering for half-hour time blocks. We can thus accommodate 12 people each evening during the course of a three-hour search session.

Statistics

Usage data on instruction and search appointments can help reveal potential problem areas in the new service, assist in planning revisions to the program, and document levels of activity. Knowing how many and what types of people are coming to the library for end-user instruction is useful in planning the content of workshops. It also serves as the basis for a comparison with the numbers and types of people who *actually search* as a result of the instructional program. When a high proportion of those who receive instruction are motivated to search, the library can be confident that its program is working. This figure is perhaps a better indicator of success than the raw total of people who take an introductory workshop, or the number who search.

We generate statistics on end-user searching from a combination of logbooks, scheduling sheets, and payment receipts. Logbooks and scheduling sheets record the number of appointments, the length of searches, the databases accessed, the amount and methods of payment, and any other information a library may choose to record about patterns of searching. By recording receipts from patrons for search charges, the library can, in conjunction with vendors' invoices, calculate the net cost of the search service. Cost figures are critical in justifying budget requests and reassessing user fees.

Costs and Billing

How should a library handle the costs associated with end-user searching? The answer to this question will depend on the library's service philosophy and on its funding sources. In a broad sense, there are three options: the library can charge users the full cost of their searches; the library can partly subsidize patron searches; or the library can provide the service without charge.

When a library provides training and search services to students enrolled in particular courses, financial support may be sought from academic departments, grants, or other sources that supplement the library's base budget. Assuming that the library will pass on all or part of the search costs, it may directly charge search costs as billed by the system or compensate for those charges by a fee structure that is simpler for the patron to understand. At our library, we have grouped the databases to which we provide access into two sets based on connect hour prices. We bill for end-user searches at the rate of either $8.00 or $20.00 per hour, depending on the database. Recently we have added citation charges for some databases. The minimum unit of time is a 15-minute block, which will cost either $2.00 or $5.00. This system allows the patron to estimate search charges in advance, and to clearly understand the consequences of extending a search.

Most libraries with end-user search programs take payment on completion of a search. Traditional methods of payment include cash, check, and departmental account number. Other vehicles of payment such as credit card, deposit account, direct billing, and "venda-card," may also merit consideration. One payment alternative, made possible by developing technology, is a vending device which attaches to the microcomputer, accepts cash, and times a search. This device removes the need for complicated billing procedures. Another alternative is made possible by systems like IAC's Search Helper. These systems provide standardized search costs that permit accurate planning and budgeting by eliminating billing surprises.

Security

The security of library hardware, software, and system passwords are a real concern. A library with an end-user search program needs to take precautions against the threat of theft and abuse. Terminals, microcomputers, and system peripherals can be bolted down, removed to a locked closet, or kept in a secure room. Software should never leave the sight or control of authorized personnel without a deposit or proper patron identification.

The protection of system passwords presents a different problem. It is difficult to protect against a determined and competent hacker, but the library can mask passwords on microcomputers by building them into "macros" within communications software. Through this technique, the communications package logs onto an online system in response to a user prompt, without exposing the log-on exchange on screen. The user then need never see the password. Another protection involves the use of transitory secondary passwords, like BRS's AMIS, which the library can change regularly.

Little stands between the abusive user and access to the system if the library uses a dumb terminal for searching. Short of saying, "Don't look!" the library cannot prevent the patron from watching during the log-in process and remembering the keystroke sequence. A new and potentially useful approach to password security involves the allocation of a number of "disposable" passwords, each valid for only one search.

INTEGRATING END-USER SEARCHING INTO ESTABLISHED LIBRARY SERVICES AND PROGRAMS

End-user searching should be an integral part of overall library programs and services. Furthermore, structuring and marketing an end-user program has major ramifications for other library services, programs and staff. A library will usually feel the immediate effect of the programs and activities associated with end-user searching at such public service contact points as reference desks and in library instruction programs, previously existing mediated online search services, interlibrary services, and collection development.

The impact can be particularly heavy on personnel at service desks who are required to understand and explain the program to the public without the benefit of having planned it. Staff members who are not directly involved in the operation of the program are important to its success, in that often they are the ones who interact with patrons on a daily basis. To help prevent unnecessary fears or concerns from developing, open lines of communication are essential. Although the library should have one individual coordinate the program, everyone on the staff who may be affected by it should be involved in some aspect of planning, evaluation, or review. The program coordinator should keep everyone informed of new developments and provide them with the information they need to interact with patrons of the search service.

Over the past several years, the professional literature has treated stress and over-extension at the reference desk. Articles by individuals such as Bunge and Miller have stated that "we seem to be spread ever more thinly," that the "expanded range of information resources all too often becomes a source of frustration,"[1] and that we are "pushing ourselves beyond our levels of comfort and competence."[2] Miller goes so far as to say that automation has increased, not decreased, the librarian's workload. What place do these professional warnings have with regard to the end-user's impact on the reference desk? A public services research project at the Evans Library, Texas A&M University, sponsored by the ARL's Office of Management Studies, concluded that:

> No library program, regardless how user-friendly it may be, is ever implemented without staff effort. Normal increases in staff workload can be expected with addition of any new reference service. The introduction of end user searching, however, it was felt might place extraordinary demand on staff members already well occupied at the reference desk.[3]

The report went on to state that although "the level of staff required to provide adequate service is not out of the range of possibility for at least moderately staffed libraries ... it is unlikely that offering end user services can be absorbed as yet another service from the reference desk."[4]

A library can secure the budget and staff necessary to insure the success of a new program from two places: existing programs and services or external funding sources. In our library, additional part-time staff resources were secured to reinforce the reference unit. This was fortunate, in that we observed an obvious increase in traffic across the reference desk as a result of our end-user program. Student searchers asked to use thesauri, sought guidance in the formulation of their search strategies, made and cancelled search appointments, completed interlibrary loan forms, and requested interpretation of their search results and assistance in locating documents within the university library system. This increase in desk activity was initially overwhelming for some staff members. For a time, we helped moderate the load by assigning an additional librarian to the desk on weekday afternoons. This librarian was on call to assist students with presearch planning: topic refinement, keyword selection, and the use of Boolean logic.

Other ways of preparing reference staff members to cope with the support of an end-user search program include an orientation for information assistants, the establishment of consistent procedures, and the identification of one individual as the contact for questions and concerns related to end-user searching. In our case, group discussions among the reference librarians also helped to improve the level of understanding and acceptance of the end-user program.

A library needs also to monitor the effect end-user searching has on its overall instructional program. Although the library should make positive efforts to include information about online resources wherever that is appropriate in its instructional program, there is a danger that a popular end-user program will drain energy from other important instructional activities. If the end-user program becomes so large that it requires additional personnel for planning and administration, the library may wish to elevate the program to the status of an independent reference service to maintain the momentum of other instructional functions.

How will end-user searching affect existing mediated search services? This will depend upon factors such as user convenience, comparative costs, system and database availability, patron information needs, and the sophistication and expectations of the user population. Patrons who have undergone end-user instruction can become more aware of the options available to them, and even grow more apt to take advantage of a librarian's searching skills and the broader array of databases and systems accessible through mediated searches than the average patron. Still, in our library, the mediated search service COMPASS has experienced a decrease in patron demand since we began our program in end-user searching. We have lost people with relatively simple search questions, who now search independently, while gaining those who realize that more information may be available than they have managed to locate on their own. Our mediated search service, while somewhat reduced in scale, is thus concentrating upon more sophisticated information needs than it was before we implemented end-user searching.

Despite the increase in traffic at the reference desk, we believe that end-user searching actually has its greatest effect on the instruction program and on staffing roles and patterns. Secondarily, there is impact on interlibrary services and collection development. While there has not appeared any conclusive research to date on the scope of this impact, our experience indicates that end-users of online systems request more material from interlibrary loan than students who search printed indexes and abstracts. While students have searched the print equivalents of these sources for years and also encountered limitations on locally available materials, they generally retrieve more references through online searches since they use more subject terms and search a longer time span than they might manually. Because of the increase in interlibrary loan requests, we occasionally encounter copyright barriers for certain publications. In some instances, demand from end-users has led us to purchase back issues of select journals, and to consider others for subscription.

FUTURE TRENDS AND PROSPECTS

It has only been within the last three to five years, with the advent of easy-to-use, menu-driven systems, that librarians have taken an active role in educating the end-user and helping more people to search online. This increase in end-user searching activity points to a "new watershed in the history of online searching: the era of the end-user."[5] It may also become the era of the library, in that "librarians and information specialists are becoming a major force in helping end-users interface with the megalibrary."[6] According to Richard Janke, librarians "will continue to play a key role in the online retrieval of information ... for many years to come."[7]

End-user searching can open new doors for the library. Our program, for example, has generated a spin-off instructional effort in the area of bibliographic file managers. This program, which is discussed in detail in the next chapter, has earned the library new credibility with the faculty. In the near future we may also treat the scientific literature itself and the publishing, indexing, and retrieval processes associated with it, in what is an increasingly broad program of instruction in "information literacy." As a first step toward this goal, we will enhance our general end-user educational program with workshops that focus on particular subjects or with database-specific seminars in which we will teach advanced searching techniques and the nuances of particular databases. Other methods of building on our basic service might include sponsorship of user groups within departments, establishment of documentation resource centers (where the library would place copies of thesauri and other search aids), and individual consultation regarding system selection, searching hardware and software, and search formulation.

When a library succeeds in establishing a solid end-user program the number and sophistication of searchers will increase as a result. Patrons will come to demand expanded services, improved access to a greater number of databases and systems, and a continually developing expertise on the behalf of the librarians who consult with them. Instruction programs will grow in size and complexity and will move away from dependence on any one online system or hardware configuration. Libraries will also begin to purchase data files for local access that will supplement and sometimes replace traditional online information resources.

The relationship between the local online catalog and the external database will receive increasing attention in the next few years. Some mechanism must be developed that will allow the user to match search results from a DIALOG or BRS search against local holdings of materials through the library online catalog. As the bibliographic file manager may serve as a "halfway house" in this process, this possibility receives further treatment in Chapter 11.

SUMMARY

1. In the early stages of establishing an end-user program, the selection of an appropriate target audience is critical. The choice of a good target audience involves several factors, including: the group's need for information retrieval online, the availability of appropriate databases, the limitations of printed sources in the group's area of interest, the level of sophistication of the group in the use of computers and information sources, funding possibilities, and campus political factors. A good question to ask is whether members of the proposed audience have an immediate need for the kinds of information they will retrieve online. If the library succeeds in choosing a good target audience, these "converts" will provide the fledgling end-user program with effective word-of-mouth publicity.

2. In seeking support and funding for an instructional program in database searching, live demonstrations to faculty members and administrators are an effective tool. The presence of the Microcomputer Center and the Online Classroom in our library has allowed us to make frequent presentations to these groups.

3. Active cooperation on the part of a vendor of an online system can make a great difference to the success of an end-user program. As many vendors now understand that library programs provide their systems with excellent exposure and publicity, the library should solicit the understanding and support of the vendor or vendors of choice. In making an initial selection of a system or systems for end-user searching, the library should work from a set of clearly articulated criteria.

4. The use of microcomputers in an end-user program opens the possibility of using sophisticated communications and gateway software packages. It also permits the library to run local applications on the machines when they are not in use for database searching. Still, it remains the case that a library can conduct a perfectly adequate instructional program in end-user searching with "dumb" terminals, if these are available and the purchase of microcomputers is not feasible. In addition to computer hardware, a classroom with telecommunications connections, a projection system, and a blackboard are desirable.

5. Most libraries will wish to designate one public services professional as the coordinator of the end-user program. This person will be responsible for planning and publicity, will undertake faculty liaison work in connection with end-user searching, will do some classroom teaching, and will involve colleagues in teaching as appropriate. A major role of the coordinator is to insure that everyone on the library staff who will be affected by the new program has the information he or she needs to function effectively and fully understands why the library is undertaking end-user searching.

6. Most programs in end-user searching will involve the scheduling of at least two types of activity--classroom workshops and hands-on search sessions. We find 90 minutes ideal for our lecture and on-screen demonstrations, though we often cannot secure this much time when we teach students in college courses.

7. While some libraries permit end-user searching whenever the library is open, others limit the hands-on component of the program to scheduled blocks of time and provide more extensive user support. We schedule end-user searches on weekday evenings. This allows us to avoid queues, to minimize impact on our mediated search services, and to provide coaches who assist patrons with their online searches.

8. A key statistic in an end-user search program is the proportion of people that have taken the introductory workshop who actually return to

perform a database search. The proportion of participants who perform repeat searches is also revealing.

9. A vital issue in any end-user program--practically and philosophically--is that of how the library will handle charges. There are three basic options: the library can charge users the full cost of their searches; the library can partly subsidize patron searches; or the library can provide end-user searching without charge. We seek college funding for courses that require students to perform database searches, and charge other users according to a simplified scale that makes costs understandable and predictable.

10. The development of an end-user program in online database searching is an ambitious undertaking for a library. The new program can affect existing instructional efforts, mediated searching services, general reference desk activity, and collection development and interlibrary loan operations. Careful planning is essential if the library is to absorb smoothly the end-user program.

11. In recent years, the library literature has treated the issue of stress at the reference desk. Before undertaking a large program of instruction and support in end-user searching, a library should evaluate staffing requirements in detail and see that the needed resources are in place. Additional part-time or student support may be valuable in certain areas. In our library, for example, student members of the staff of the Microcomputer Center work as coaches in the hands-on component of our end-user program. We assigned an additional librarian to the reference desk on weekday afternoons to help with the consulting load generated by end-user searching. A library should not allow a popular end-user searching program to destroy the overall integrity of its instructional program.

12. A library should anticipate that an end-user program will affect its existing search services. While demand for mediated search services in our library, for instance, has dropped somewhat since the implementation of end-user searching, in some cases an introduction to database searching makes patrons better aware of the full spectrum of search services that the library offers. Our mediated service now seems to be answering a more uniform need for sophisticated search support, as end-users begin to perform simple searches by themselves. Interlibrary loan and collection development have felt an increase in demand for materials as a result of end-user searching in our library.

13. Despite the challenges and difficulties, the advent of computerized information systems driven by menus or simple command structures presents libraries with an excellent opportunity to increase the scope of their instructional offerings, and to address, in a comprehensive fashion, the need of students today for a thoroughgoing program in "information literacy."

Notes

1. Charles A. Bunge, "Potential and Reality at the Reference Desk: Reflections on a 'Return to the Field'," *Journal of Academic Librarianship* 10(3): 128-33 (July 1984).

2. William Miller, "What's Wrong with Reference?: Coping with Success and Failure at the Reference Desk," *American Libraries* 15(5): 303-6, 321-22 (May 1984).

3. Jane Dodd, Charles Gilreath, and Geraldine Hutchins, *A Comparison of Two End User Operated Search Systems* (Washington, D.C.: ARL Office of Management Studies, 1985).

4. Ibid., p.33.

5. Barbara Quint, "From the Editor," *Database End-User* 1(1): 3 (July/August 1985).

6. Jack W. Simpson, "The Inverted File: Guest Editorial; Information Megatrends," *Online* 9(2): 7 (March 1985).

7. Richard V. Janke, "Client Searchers and Intermediaries: The New Online Partnership," in *Online '85; Conference Proceedings, 11/4-6/85* (Weston, Conn.: Online, Inc., 1985), pp. 165-71.

Chapter 11

Teaching Users to Manage Their Own Databases

Katherine Chiang and Linda Stewart

PERSONAL FILE MANAGEMENT AND RESEARCH FACULTY

Instruction in bibliographic file management--the control of literature references with a microcomputer--is a natural extension of the library's end-user searching program. Some of those who attend our workshops in online database searching will subsequently search on their own machines, and will want to download search results and incorporate them into personal literature files. This is particularly true of faculty and research personnel who currently maintain a manual reprint file.

Since mid-1984, library staff members have collected bibliographic management programs, evaluated them, distributed the evaluations within the university, and written software reviews for publication. We decided a workshop would be another effective way to disseminate the information we gather to the Cornell faculty. The library views this as an extension of its traditional role of instruction in the use of bibliographic indexes and abstracts in both print and online formats.

Bibliographic file managers are programs either specifically designed for, or capable of controlling, bibliographic records. They mix database management and text-editing functions. Bibliographic file managers allow the entry and modification of long blocks of text, as would a text editor, and handle fields like a database manager.

The most sophisticated programs perform a wide range of functions related to bibliographic control. They allow the user to type records at the keyboard or to batch load records produced under another program or downloaded from an online database. These programs support searches of the local database, retrieving individual or sets of logically grouped records. Some programs search the contents of the database itself, taking several minutes or longer; others maintain complex indexes which allow a 1,000-record database to be searched in seconds. Bibliographic file managers can print out the citations retrieved from a search according to user specifications. Some programs can work with the texts of manuscripts written with a word processor, thus allowing the integration, in effect, of the writing of a paper and the citation-management function.

Those in academia familiar with the online bibliographic databases, and with word-processing or database management software, realized the potential of the microcomputer for handling personal literature files some time ago. Even before the first bibliographic file managers appeared, faculty members at Cornell were asking librarians if programs to handle citations existed. The programs that have subsequently appeared on the market were written for diverse audiences. Their functions and quality vary widely. Faculty members stand the risk of making a costly mistake if they choose a bibliographic file manager without first developing an understanding of their own needs and the spectrum of software packages now on the market. Although it takes time and energy to evaluate these programs as they emerge, we felt the library should take on that responsibility and serve as a campus clearinghouse for this genre of software.

CAPABILITIES OF BIBLIOGRAPHIC FILE MANAGEMENT PACKAGES

As mentioned above, bibliographic file managers reflect the needs of different interest groups including information brokers, bibliographers, and publishing academics. Although each package has its individual strengths and weaknesses, we have focused on products which can perform the three major functions of input, searching, and formatted output.

Input

The basic unit of a database is the record--a bibliographic reference. Records are generally subdivided into fields, such as author, title, and date of publication. Some programs handle only bibliographic citations and have defined sets of fields. Others allow the user to design record structures. Because of the flexibility this permits, packages that do permit the user to create a record structure should perhaps be considered "text-oriented database managers," as opposed to simply "bibliographic file managers." We treat the two together here.

Once the structure of the database is established, the user can either type citations record by record or load them in batch from another machine-readable source (downloaded citations or a file of references created with a text editor). The user usually must reformat records to conform to the field structure of the bibliographic file manager, although some file managers will, for example, automatically reformat bibliographic records taken from certain online databases.

Entering individual records from the keyboard is straightforward. Programs will prompt the user for entry by displaying a template that accommodates an entire record, or proceed on a field-by-field basis. The strongest programs in this area have full-screen editors and resemble word processors in flexibility.

Searching

Most bibliographic management packages provide some means of retrieving an individual record or set of records from the local database. Packages differ in search capabilities, speed, and ease of use.

The need for a powerful search function will depend on the size of the local database and the familiarity of the user with the records in the file. Someone working with a large departmental database that contains citations he or she did not input may require a powerful search language, while a single researcher who constructs a personal reprint file of familiar articles may be content with crude author and title searches. The most elegant packages usually mimic the commercial online services, which manage millions of records. Useful search features include:

1. Boolean operators: (*AND*, *OR*, and *NOT*).

2. Nesting: Several Boolean operators may be used in one search command, with the user able to specify, usually by means of parentheses, which operations are to be performed first.

3. Set manipulation: The results of searches are saved for later recall, or for combination with subsequent sets.

4. Phrase searching: Multi-word phrases can be searched.

5. Truncation: One may search for word stems or parts of words.

6. Field qualification: Search statements may be limited to specific data elements, such as titles or keywords.

7. Weighting: The user is able to assign some search terms more importance in the search than others. In sophisticated packages, the user can

distinguish between sets of references containing all or most of the search terms and sets containing only a few.

Search speed is important with large databases. Packages that create indexes are generally fast, as are those that provide the capability to search a designated field.

Ease of use is important to untrained or infrequent searchers. Menus, tutorials, and help screens can serve as aids; however, command-driven packages are often faster and more flexible.

Output

Some users will want to generate bibliographies conforming to a specific style. Information brokers, for example, will require attractive products to distribute, while authors who are submitting articles to several journals may need to convert their bibliographies to the differing specifications of the various publications. In these cases, the user will want the capability to finely control the formatting of output for subsequent use. Some packages print records only as they have been stored in the database; others allow citations to be saved to a text file where the user can modify them with word-processing software.

The degree of control over printed output depends in part on the original design of the database records. Since most software packages permit some control over the order of fields in a printout, units of data that need to be manipulated on output should be isolated in discrete fields.

Some packages can perform global changes on records to be output, such as rearrangement of field order, the deletion of field tags, or the addition of punctuation or words such as "Edited by" at the beginning or end of fields. Some packages permit alterations to individual records as well. Records can be scrolled across the screen, as in a word processor, and editorial changes introduced. This is time consuming, but useful where changes must be made at unpredictable points or *within* fields. In certain cases, sets of records from several files, or records with different structures (such as books and journal articles), can be merged into one list on output. The ideal package would probably support if/then programming--the ability to "test" each record and manipulate it in a particular way depending on the result of the test.

Sophisticated packages designed for authors and academics allow close interaction with a word processor, so that the tasks of producing a manuscript and generating a corresponding bibliography may proceed together. The bibliographic manager extracts those citations from the database that correspond to references in the text file, creating a bibliography for a scientific paper or journal article.

WORKSHOPS IN BIBLIOGRAPHIC FILE MANAGEMENT

Overview

In June 1984 two Public Services librarians in our library taught a three-hour workshop on the use of bibliographic file managers for controlling personal literature files in the same program for Cornell faculty members as described in previous chapters. The session was organized around three packages. The instructors introduced the functions of each program and participants worked with each in turn on the machines in the Microcomputer Center's classroom.

When we offered the workshop to a faculty audience for a second time in January 1985, several more packages had appeared on the market. Still, none possessed all the features we wanted in a bibliographic file manager. We again presented an overview of the field, rather than trying to push the audience toward a particular package. We decided it would not be productive to describe all the programs then available. Instead, we concentrated on describing the characteristic features of bibliographic file managers. Participants could decide which functions were most important for them and choose the program that most closely matched their needs. In addition to the program for faculty, we have included bibliographic file management in our series of open workshops.

As mentioned in Chapter 3, Mann Library collects bibliographic file managers at a comprehensive level. Thus, participants in the workshop could supplement what was learned in the session with further individual experimentation with the packages in the Microcomputer Center's collection.

Goals of the Workshop

The purpose of the bibliographic file management workshop is to familiarize participants with the criteria for selecting a program that will organize their personal files of bibliographic references. We have established the following goals for the three-hour session:

1. Participants, using guidelines discussed by the presenters, are able to assess their own needs for a reprint or bibliographic management system.

2. Participants can list data elements they would like included in each bibliographic record.

3. Participants can distinguish major options in file management systems (menu-driven versus command-driven, "generic text-oriented database manager" versus bibliographic file manager, user-designed output formats versus system-determined formats) and can enumerate the respective advantages and disadvantages of these features.

4. Participants can complete file management exercises in the areas of input, searching, and output.

Content of the Workshops

The sessions in bibliographic file management are broken into several segments. A general introduction is followed by a needs assessment exercise in which participants consider the characteristics desired in their files, as well as the hardware, software, financial, and personnel resources they have available. We explain the basic notions of record design and vocabulary control, using examples from commercial bibliographic systems. Next, we use a flowchart to present a conceptual model for the establishment of a system on a microcomputer. Finally, the significant functions of file management systems--input, searching, and output--are discussed, sample packages are demonstrated, and participants perform hands-on exercises-- usually one exercise per function. We encourage participants to compare software for flexibility, speed, and ease of use.

TEACHING EXPERIENCES

Preparation for the workshops in bibliographic file management involved selecting and learning to use the software packages we would teach, developing materials, and publicity. We relied on reviews and product announcements in the published literature as well as the recommendations of faculty members in making our original selection of packages. Demonstration versions of many systems can be secured at a reasonable cost and are usually adequate to the purposes of classroom instruction.

As new packages appear on the market, we have grown more selective in our preparation for the workshop. Learning to use the packages initially requires much staff time, although learning one system thoroughly makes learning subsequent ones easier. Access to computer facility staff members who can help with questions about general microcomputer operation is invaluable.

The faculty program in microcomputing is publicized through the Dean of the Faculty's office. For the open workshops, we have undertaken publicity through both Cornell Computer Services and library channels, including bulletin board announcements and mailings. We have found that it is important to be clear that the workshop emphasizes the selection of software for bibliographic references; some participants are more interested in managing other types of files. The announcements specify which hardware configurations we will cover. Our workshops have emphasized the IBM PC partly because it is readily available in our facility and partly because most bibliographic management software has been written for the IBM machine and compatibles. Packages for the Apple Macintosh, the other machine in wide use at Cornell, are just beginning to appear.

Our instructional materials consist of handouts and diskettes. The handouts include:

1. An outline of activities for the class.
2. A sample bibliographic record from a BRS database with fields labelled.
3. A list of thesauri available in the library, which participants may examine to familiarize themselves with such features as controlled vocabulary and concept codes.
4. A flowchart diagramming the input, search, and output functions of bibliographic management software.
5. A comparison chart evaluating the packages we have examined.

Preparation of the diskettes for a workshop involves obtaining permission from the vendor to use multiple copies of a program in demonstration or complete versions, designing demonstrations and exercises that will illustrate the essential functions of the packages, and creating sample files. Finally, we must duplicate, test, label, and distribute the diskettes to each workstation.

The workshop lasts three hours. The hands-on exercises cause the most problems during the sessions. Participants are extremely varied in their microcomputer experience and typing ability. Some need considerable individual attention, while others prefer a rapid pace. Machines sometimes malfunction and diskettes may inexplicably fail. Although we usually run the sessions with two professionals, an optimal number of instructors with a workshop of 20 people would be four--one to lecture, one to operate the instructor's microcomputer, and two to assist individual participants.

WORKSHOP EVALUATION

Our general evaluation of the workshops has sought to answer three questions:

1. Who is coming to the sessions?
2. How useful have they found the program?
3. What future activities are they planning in the area of bibliographic file management?

In trying to characterize our audience, we relied on two sources--sign-up sheets passed around the classroom during the session and evaluation forms distributed afterward. Our information derives from five sessions held in 1985, attended by 59 people. Two workshops held earlier and one 1985 workshop restricted to the library staff were not analyzed.

Most participants were faculty members, partly because, for three of the workshops, attendance was restricted to that group. It is also true, however, that faculty have a more pressing need for automated management of reprint files than do other groups. By subject area, attendance broke down as follows:

71 percent life sciences
18.6 percent social sciences
10.4 percent other, including all humanities, food science, engineering, and library staff.

The interest of the program to life science researchers was especially marked. Although Mann Library specializes in the life sciences and certain social sciences, the workshops were available to, and publicized to, the entire Cornell community.

We attempted to ascertain previous computer experience with a general question on our sign-up sheet. Some participants responded by listing hardware they had used, others by mentioning tasks (e.g., word processing) they had performed with a computer. One obvious trend was that the number of people answering "none" or "minimal" decreased steadily over the six-month period--from 40.0 percent to 7.1 percent.

Questions on the evaluation sheet distributed at the last three workshops were designed to assess our audience's interests. While most (20 respondents) intended to manage their own personal bibliographic files, six were charged with planning systems for their departments, research teams, or laboratories.

Since the packages we have examined have their respective strengths and weaknesses, we wanted to see which functions our audience considered most desirable. Participants were asked to rate the following:

1. Downloading or importing downloaded records.
2. Manually inputting records.
3. Searching the bibliographic database.
4. Printing output according to specification.

Participants were able to assign the following weights to the four areas: Irrelevant, Low Priority, Preferred, High Priority, or Essential. Interestingly, the function accorded the highest priority, on the average, was Manual Input, while Downloading received the lowest. Perhaps participants were more interested in managing references they already had than in obtaining new ones from external databases. It is also possible that most researchers do not yet understand the full potential of combining online searching with local reference management.

We were also interested to learn whether powerful search capability or flexible output was the more highly valued feature. We found that slightly more than one-third of our sample rated searching and output as equal in priority, the same number rated searching as more important than output, while somewhat less than one-third rated output the more important. There does not seem to be a clear preference for one of these two functions.

We stated during the needs assessment portion of the workshop that users should seriously consider investing the time and money required to construct a local database, but that one acceptable result of the workshop might be to dissuade them from establishing a system at this time. Through responses to our question about their future plans, however, we learned that most participants left the program expecting to implement a system--18 of 26 were considering purchasing file management software, and five others planned to use software they already owned.

EXPANDING THE LIBRARIAN'S ROLE

The comments of the participants in our workshops, and the overall success of the program, prove that an audience exists at Cornell for instruction in bibliographic file management. This should hold true at any institution where a significant proportion of faculty members conduct research. We believe that demand among faculty and researchers for instruction and consulting support in the creation of automated reprint files will increase rapidly for the next several years. After that point, when most of the faculty members who use a computer and want to automate their reprint files have actually managed to do so, the pressure may slacken somewhat. We anticipate, however, that graduate students will begin to construct personal bibliographic files, as may undergraduates who are working on senior projects.

Our intent in teaching these classes was twofold: to offer patrons formal instruction in the evaluation and use of the bibliographic file managers, and to establish our library as the campus consulting resource for these programs. We have now met both goals.

Faculty members and graduate students who have taken our workshop often come back to talk to us about the specifics of their situation or to ask for advice on particular software packages. Word-of-mouth referrals also bring to us individuals who have not taken the course.

Developing an intermediate level of support for patrons, to fall between the introductory workshop and one-on-one consultation, may be our next step. Once patrons decide they would like to automate their bibliographic files, they should work with programs to select the one that best meets their needs. A software open house would be one way to provide people with this experience. If we ran several copies each of three or four programs on the machines in the Microcomputer Center's classroom, patrons could circulate and compare bibliographic managers with the assistance of instructors. As the ideal configuration would be one instructor per program, this would be a labor intensive class, but it might work to reduce our consulting load.

The formal instructional program and consulting are only two aspects of our work with bibliographic file management software. As previously noted, the library collects bibliographic file management programs at a comprehensive level, in either demonstration or working versions. Naturally, as we obtain new programs we examine them and add the results to our file of software evaluations. We also work with programs in beta test sent by vendors who have learned of our commitment to this genre of software. As information specialists, we are in a position to suggest changes and improvements to the software producers. We have tried to disseminate our findings to a wide audience through published reviews and general seminars.

We view the library's activities in instruction, consulting, and the evaluation of bibliographic file management software as long-term commitments. The library is interested in playing a similar role with expert system packages, which are appearing for use with microcomputers. Clearly, the services we have begun to provide in this area parallel to some degree the offerings of Cornell Computer Services. There is no duplication in that we have an understanding with Computer Services that we will handle the area of bibliographic management packages. Though the technical vehicle is the computer, what we are instructing our patrons in is the organization and control of information. This is a field the library has worked in for years.

In addition to "spreading the word" on the power of bibliographic file management programs, we are working to change the perception patrons hold of our role as librarians, bringing this perception into line with what we actually do. Patrons come to realize that our expertise extends to handling information in any format, not just print. A proven ability to control information electronically, and to teach the university community how this is done, increases the credibility of the libraries. This is politically essential in our environment, as the Cornell libraries proceed to automate their operations and to seek the financial support necessary to purchase and implement complex computer-based systems.

THE FUTURE OF BIBLIOGRAPHIC MANAGEMENT WITH A MICROCOMPUTER

At this time, the better bibliographic file management packages provide a powerful tool for the local control of databases of literature citations. They are already more than adequate to the management of a researcher's personal reprint file. In addition, these packages are beginning to provide reasonable interfaces to external bibliographic databases, where scholars, or librarians, can perform literature searches. In some cases, as remarked earlier, bibliographic file managers also provide interfaces to the word-processing software that a scholar might use to write articles.

We believe that the next logical step in the evolution of this software is integration with library information systems. When one downloads the results of a database search, loads these citations into a local bibliographic database, and then identifies a set of important citations, the question becomes one of securing the actual documents. At present, a scholar who wanted to run a set of citations identified on a microcomputer-based system against the online catalog in a university library, to determine what is held locally, would in all probability have to search each citation against the online catalog by inputting queries from the keyboard of a library terminal.

As more people in university communities come to maintain their own bibliographic files, this bottleneck will appear increasingly unacceptable. It should be possible to identify a set of citations under the bibliographic management software and then to run these results as a batch query of the library catalog from the researcher's microcomputer, with the details of the operation transparent to the user. Furthermore, it should be possible to download citations from the library's online catalog to one's personal bibliographic database.

The development of such an interface will not be a trivial task, and may have to wait on further maturation of the library automation marketplace on the one hand and of the vendors and developers of bibliographic management software for microcomputers on the other. We believe, however, that as academics and researchers come to better understand the potential of automated information-retrieval technology, and to develop personal bibliographic files, the pressure for these interfaces will grow.

With the new generation of intelligent workstations, the bibliographic utilities are trying to move some of the computing load on their systems to microprocessors, and, at the same time, to provide libraries with increased local processing power and flexibility. Yet, from the standpoint of the academic who uses a university library, the critical development is not the cataloger's workstation but the so-called scholar's workstation. This should include the capability to access national and international information systems, to retrieve information from these sources, to manage this information locally, and to provide a reasonably seamless interface with a library's integrated library system.

SUMMARY

1. An instructional program in the use of bibliographic file managers--software programs designed to control literature citations--is a natural offshoot of end-user training in the searching of online databases. Most faculty members and researchers maintain reprint files. When they have learned to search databases and to download search results, they want to develop computerized control over their local files as well.

2. Bibliographic file managers support three major functions:
The ability to create a bibliographic database, either from entries input at the keyboard or from source files of citations derived from another database or downloaded to diskette during the course of an online search.

The ability to search the database and retrieve a set of records.

The ability to control output in order to produce an acceptable printed bibliography. This typically requires that the user be able to select a subset of the fields in a record structure for output and be able to determine the order in which fields appear.

3. A workshop is an effective method of disseminating introductory information about bibliographic file managers. Systematic software evaluations, made available to library patrons, and demonstrations to campus users groups and other computer organizations are alternative methods.

4. An important goal of a workshop in bibliographic file management is to give participants enough exposure to the capabilities of this software that they can decide whether the use of such a package is sensible for them. In our program, we also seek to bring participants to the point where they can work independently with the demonstration versions in the Microcomputer Center's collection, should they need to decide which package best suits their needs.

5. In addition to developing instructional materials and publicizing the sessions, preparation of a workshop program will require that the library staff select and learn to use bibliographic file managers. This dictates the investment of considerable staff time, but can substantially enhance the computer skills of public service professionals.

6. During instructional sessions, hands-on exposure to the software is valuable for participants. Adequate staff support should be available to prevent frustration and to keep the group working at a reasonable pace.

7. As time passes, workshops in bibliographic file management will attract people with increased exposure to microcomputing. They will be interested in locating a software package with powerful search capabilities and flexible output functions. Nevertheless, most participants in our workshops still come unaware that it is possible to import the results of an online search into a bibliographic file manager.

8. A thoroughgoing program in bibliographic file management with a microcomputer would include the following components:
Exposure in a workshop setting to the features of several software packages.

A set of criteria, flexible enough to accommodate individual needs, that allows researchers to narrow the field of software packages to a number they can realistically examine in detail.

A structured procedure for review of a given bibliographic file manager to determine whether it does meet an individual's requirements.

9. An important long-range goal of a program in bibliographic file management is to prepare the research community, and library staff, for the development of the "scholar's workstation." The scholar's workstation will eventually allow the researcher to retrieve information from on-campus and remote information systems, to manage this information locally, and to use the processing power of the microcomputer in interactions with the library's online catalog.

Chapter 12

Teaching Applications Software

Howard Curtis

APPLICATIONS SOFTWARE IN THE INFORMATION ENVIRONMENT

Since its inception, the Information Technology Section has played a major role in computer instruction at Mann Library. One component of this activity is a series of workshops in applications software. As is true of the Public Services program in the searching of online databases, described in Chapter 9, the Information Technology Section has conducted some of its workshops for student audiences within particular courses in the colleges we serve, while others have been open sessions for which any member of the university community may register.

In addition to teaching workshops in the use of applications software for student and faculty audiences, the ITS provides microcomputer instruction and support for library staff. Though we often adapt staff workshops to the special needs of our audience, we base these sessions on the same approach to teaching the use of microcomputer software that we use with external audiences. The focus of this chapter will thus be the Information Technology Section's program of workshops, for all audiences. Chapter 13 will take up mechanisms of staff support that go beyond classroom instruction.

As was suggested in Chapter 8, the subject matter of these workshops in applications software does not derive as directly from the library's commitment to teach information retrieval and control as do our workshops in online searching and bibliographic file management. In a sense, we are supplementing the instructional offerings of Cornell Computer Services for the benefit of our own college clientele. Our workshops in "generic" microcomputer applications, however, do fulfill a promise we made when we secured funding for the construction of the Microcomputer Center.

A further reason why a library may wish to teach standard applications software packages was also introduced in Chapter 8. As vendors distribute more research data on diskette, or as universities come to distribute their own data in this format, certain common software packages, such as dBase and Lotus, have emerged as standard mechanisms of access to the kinds of information that may legitimately reside in the collections of a research library. These applications packages are thus coming into their own in the field of scholarly information, as well as playing their already well-established role in the control of administrative and business data.

To date, the Information Technology Section's instructional sessions have been separate, in both subject matter and teaching personnel, from the Public Services workshops in online searching and reprint file management. We have tried to avoid giving our patrons the sense that the library runs two programs by publicizing all open workshops in the same mailings and by conducting registration through one mechanism. On several occasions, staff members of the two units have also worked together to put on a workshop.

The library is currently reexamining the spectrum of services that it offers patrons. In the area of computer-based instruction we may decide to concentrate our resources more narrowly on the set of activities that are clearly related to information access, retrieval, and local control. We also may decide to continue our workshops in applications software but to integrate the teaching activities of the Public Services unit and the Information Technology Section more thoroughly.

WORKSHOPS IN APPLICATIONS SOFTWARE

The Information Technology Section has structured four workshops to date--a general introduction to the IBM PC and the DOS operating system; a session on WordPerfect, the word-processing program used most widely at Cornell; an introduction to spreadsheets using Multiplan, and, more recently, Lotus; and a workshop in database management that employs the popular "freeware" package PC-File III. We conduct these sessions in the Microcomputer Center's classroom, as they all include extensive hands-on practice with the programs. The workshops range from two to three-and-a-half hours in length.

Although in each workshop we use a particular application package, we try to teach the material at a conceptual as well as a practical level, so that participants emerge with an understanding they can apply to the operation of other software packages of the same type. This conceptual approach to the subject is particularly true of the workshop on spreadsheets, where each package that belongs to the genre shares an obvious set of logical characteristics.

With the exception of faculty workshops, where we limit enrollment to 20, we allow 35 people to register for our workshops in applications software. High attendance sometimes results in participants working in pairs on several of the microcomputers in the Microcomputer Center classroom, but, as attendance is usually lower than the number of people who sign up for a workshop, permitting overenrollment does assure us a reasonably full house for each session.

Our experience in teaching the workshops in applications software has led us to modify their content substantially. For example, we dropped the general introduction to the microcomputer entirely after several months of teaching. The purpose of this workshop was to acquaint participants with the principal components of a microcomputer system, placing special emphasis on the keyboard, and then to introduce them to the concepts of a program, an operating system, and a "file" as a logical entity. The workshop ended with a series of exercises in the manipulation of files under the disk operating system.

We soon came to the conclusion that we were putting the conceptual cart before the practical horse. Until someone has worked with at least one application package, the notions of program and file and their relationships to the microcomputer hardware are too vague to function as working knowledge. We now give a brief sketch of the overall logic of a microcomputer system at the beginning of each of our workshops, take the operation of an application package as our real point of departure, and work from this concrete experience back into the concepts of program and file.

The Information Technology Section's workshop in word processing will serve as an illustration of what we attempt to achieve in our instruction for faculty members and students. The overview of a microcomputer system that begins the session does not require that workshop participants have prior computer experience. Rather we are trying to bring everyone, no matter what their background, to the point where they can conceptually relate the different hardware components of a system. We stress the relationship between machine memory and diskette storage, in order to communicate the importance of saving one's work. Next we present the concept that the system hardware, operating system, application program, and user data constitute a hierarchy in which each succeeding element rests on a base composed of the lower-level building blocks. The instructor then spends about ten minutes describing the keyboard of the IBM PC in some detail, because of its obvious importance in word processing. At this time, we point out that the ten function keys on the keyboard play different roles under different applications programs, without taking up their particular use within the program that we treat in this workshop--WordPerfect.

During the next half hour, the workshop focuses on WordPerfect, beginning with a typing exercise that serves to convince participants that it is not terribly difficult to "get started." This is followed with practice in moving the cursor and making simple insertions, deletions, and corrections. Through this exercise we also introduce the idea that spaces and carriage returns are "real" entities within a document. The instructor then explains how the function keys operate in WordPerfect and how one may use the plastic keyboard overlay as a reference to their behavior. Participants familiarize themselves with the operation of the function keys by underlining, bolding, and centering text. Since the keyboard template represents one level of reference material or program documentation, the instructor takes this opportunity to describe the printed WordPerfect manual and to demonstrate the interactive help facility, which constitute the other major reference sources for the program.

At this point, participants all have text on screen to work with, and we take up the saving and retrieval of files. Although the procedures we use are necessarily specific to WordPerfect, we return the discussion to the more general concepts we sketched at the beginning of the workshop. It is much more important that students come away from the workshop with a grasp of what a file on diskette is, and how it relates to the current contents of the RAM-based editor, than it is that they memorize the various sequences of keystrokes and commands that we take them through under WordPerfect.

We want participants to understand what "saving your work" really means when using a microcomputer. If participants leave the workshop with this conceptual understanding, we feel we have succeeded, even though they may have to refer to the documentation the next time they use the program to recall the details of saving a document. To reinforce participants' grasp of the notions of saving and retrieving files, and to clarify the complexities of these operations under WordPerfect, we distinguish among a number of cases: saving a document when one wants next to work on another document, saving a document when one is through with a WordPerfect work session, and saving a document periodically for the sake of safety when one is writing a long document.

After a ten-minute coffee break, the workshop resumes with an exercise based upon a "highly formatted" poem by e.e. cummings, which introduces the concept of embedded codes. We again state the notion that spaces, tabs, and carriage returns, though not visible on the editor screen, are entities in a file just as is the letter X. What follows is a demonstration of how the formatting functions students have learned, such as underlining, are supported by embedded codes, and how these codes may be inserted and deleted in a document. We point out that this mechanism for controlling text is not unique to WordPerfect but general to many word processors and text editors.

The next exercise has participants edit a longer document than they have seen heretofore, allowing us to review the techniques of modifying text and to explore the behavior of "page breaks." We then have students retrieve a second document in such a way as to append it to the end of the first document. One objective here is to further clarify the relationship between disk storage, individual documents, and the editor.

The second document retrieved is single-spaced, in contrast to the first, which is double-spaced, and has wider margin settings. We proceed to adjust these parameters to produce a uniform whole. Participants then move a paragraph from the bottom to the top of the new document, invoking the MOVE function, and add a title--centered, bolded, and underlined. At the close of the workshop, as time allows, we demonstrate the WordPerfect spelling checker and techniques for printing one's work. Participants are often particularly impressed by the potential of a spelling checker and interactive thesaurus.

This word-processing workshop has several general objectives. First, we seek to give participants an overall understanding of a microcomputer system and the interrelationships of its components, with special emphasis on diskette storage and RAM memory. While acknowledging the impossibility of covering a complex software package in three hours, we want participants at least to gain confidence that they can produce a simple document and modify its contents. Third, we try to introduce concepts such as file storage, file retrieval, and embedded codes, in such a way that participants are able to transport what they have learned to similar software packages. Our other workshops extend these principles to spreadsheet and database management software.

There is enormous potential in all these sessions, given the strong hands-on orientation, for confusion at a trivial level. People will insert their diskettes into a disk drive upside down or forget to depress the "Alt" key before they strike "F4." Such mistakes may cause the individual to fall behind the group and grow frustrated. While trying to sort out what went wrong, the participant ceases to listen to the instructor and falls further behind.

One solution to this problem is to provide coaches in the classroom. Whenever possible, we involve three staff members in our workshops. Frequently, one instructor may be presenting material to the group and another demonstrating the procedure on the machine linked to our video display system. This arrangement leaves one instructor free to roam the classroom and assist participants who are encountering problems. We also structure the workshops so that there are periods of intensive hands-on activity, and periods when participants are not working with their machines but listening to a presentation about saving a file, embedded codes, or whatever the topic at hand may be. When we have the attention of the entire group, we can discuss issues of substance and be assured people are not distracted because they have hit the wrong key. When participants have absorbed the concept, we then encourage them to give the procedure a try with the machine. The constant challenge of these workshops is to provide hands-on experience while retaining a focus that is at all conceptual.

WORKSHOPS FOR LIBRARY STAFF

The opening of the Microcomputer Center gave us the physical facilities to undertake formal instruction for library staff in the use of microcomputers. The Information Technology Section has offered training in the productivity software currently in use in the library--primarily word processing, spreadsheets, and file management packages--when usage of the Microcomputer Center is otherwise light--in January, during the week of spring break, and over the summer months. In addition, the Public Services Department has put on special sessions of its workshops in online searching and bibliographic file management for staff.

The library has offered both workshops limited to the staff of Mann Library and two large training programs for the Cornell University library system. The first of these programs, undertaken in conjunction with the library personnel office in July 1984, addressed the needs of support staff. The goals of the program were to provide a general introduction to microcomputer systems, to give participants exposure to one application package, and to demonstrate to the administration of the library system the degree of interest in microcomputing within the staff and the need to provide additional workstations for staff use.

Each participant in this program for support staff attended two workshops within a two-week period. The first session consisted of our introductory workshop--an overview of the operation of the IBM PC and of file manipulation under the operating system. In the second workshop, participants learned to use the word processor WordPerfect, the spreadsheet Multiplan, or the file manager PC-File. Staff members chose among these three options according to their personal preference when they registered for the program with the personnel office.

We had anticipated a favorable response to the publicity for the program, given the interest in microcomputing around the Cornell campus, but registration exceeded our expectations. In all, 129 members of the library support staff registered for the workshops. They did so at a time when, outside the Microcomputer Center itself, there were fewer than ten microcomputers in place in the Cornell library system. One result of the program was to highlight the contrast between the interest in microcomputers in the libraries and their potential, on the one hand, and the lack of hardware in the libraries to support microcomputer-based projects.

In January 1985, the Information Technology Section worked with the library Professional Development Committee to put on a program of workshops for librarians. We covered the same types of software--word processing, spreadsheets, and database managers--that we had in the sessions for our support staff, but the structure of this program differed considerably. By this time, we had decided that the introduction to the microcomputer was not an effective workshop, for the reasons related earlier in this chapter. Instead we gave a rapid overview of system components and organization in a workshop that treated a specific application package. Staff members could thus choose sessions in word processing, spreadsheets, or database management, without the need to take a generic introduction. The first workshop consisted of intensive hands-on practice with one application package. In the second session of each of the three units of the program, library staff members who had used the software under consideration in their work demonstrated their application with the projection system in the Microcomputer Center's classroom and discussed their project. These presentations included, for example, an acquisitions system written in dBase III for use in the Rare Books Department and spreadsheet systems developed to maintain circulation and interlibrary loan statistics. The demonstrations gave staff members who had accomplished something with a microcomputer a forum to explain their projects, lent a practical focus to what people had learned in the first workshop, and encouraged participants to put their new skills to work in their own libraries.

In summary, although teaching applications software is perhaps not central to the achievement of our library's goals in establishing a program of instruction in information literacy, we have filled a need in the general area of computer literacy within our colleges. Teaching applications software has gained the library credibility with both students and faculty. It has served as a vehicle to strengthen our relationship with Cornell Computer Services. In addition, as argued above and in Chapter 8, certain standard applications packages are coming to play a significant role in accessing scholarly information.

In order to teach applications software effectively, a library will need to be able to make use of a computer facility, though that facility need not necessarily be under the library's control. In addition, a library with an interest in undertaking a program of this kind should consider: (1) whether there is substantial demand for the type of instruction that the library is contemplating, (2) whether the library has the staff and the expertise to offer instruction in applications software, (3) what the relationship will be between these instructional sessions and any programs in information access and control that the library may offer, (4) how the library's offerings will complement those of the campus computing center. At many universities today, the use of software on a microcomputer is a target of opportunity. There is a great demand for practical instruction in the application of microcomputers that the academic department of computer science may not be willing to address. The staff of the computing center may find itself overwhelmed by the sudden rush to microcomputing, coupled with the continuing presence of mainframe computing demand that will not disappear. If the library can secure the resources to offer instruction in microcomputer software, it stands to gain general credibility for its programs and valuable expertise for its staff that can be applied to in-house microcomputer projects and training.

SUMMARY

1. Certain common applications packages are becoming standard mechanisms of access to data distributed on microcomputer diskette. Although our workshops in the use of microcomputer applications software started with a commitment on the part of the library to the support of general computer literacy programs within our constituent colleges, this development may cause us to bring these workshops more fully into the fold of our training program in information access, retrieval, and control.

2. A library must consider what spectrum of applications software it is willing to teach and what its approach will be. We have taught workshops in word processing, spreadsheets, and database management. We have also offered an overall introduction to the IBM PC and the MS/PC-DOS operating system. As a result of these efforts, we have concluded that it is not practical to teach the "general" concepts of a program or a file on diskette until students have gained experience with at least one applications package. A very brief overview of the components of a microcomputer system at the beginning of a workshop is usually sufficient introduction, even for novices. Work with the application in question then provides the basis to introduce the notions of program and file.

3. In workshops in applications software it is important to stress the relationship between machine memory and diskette storage, particularly as it pertains to saving files. In our workshop in word processing, we also

present the concept that the system hardware, operating system, application program, and user data form a logical hierarchy. In addition to bringing participants to the point where they can create a simple document under a particular word processor, we try to familiarize them with mechanisms, such as "embedded codes," that are common to many programs. A major goal in all software workshops should be to convey a set of concepts that can be carried from one program to another within the same category of software.

4. Hands-on computer workshops present the constant danger that participants will fall behind the group and grow frustrated because of trivial keyboard errors. A library can minimize these problems by providing coaches in the classroom and by alternating between structured presentations by an instructor and hands-on work.

5. A library microcomputer center opens the possibility of conducting a formal program of computer instruction for a library staff. In addition to improving staff computer skills, this allows the library to make the most efficient use of the time of its computer support personnel.

6. Teaching applications software is an excellent way for a library to gain credibility and to foster cooperation with the campus computing center. The danger in undertaking such a program is that demand will prove so great that the library will lose its traditional focus on scholarly information.

Chapter 13

The Support of Microcomputer Use by Library Staff

Howard Curtis

With the remarkable increase in processing power and the almost equally remarkable decline in prices that has characterized the microcomputer marketplace over the last three years, even diehard doubters have conceded the potential of microcomputer technology to assist in library operations. Still, despite obvious advances in the "user interface," microcomputers remain challenging and often frustrating tools. As outlined in the previous chapter, a microcomputer center allows a library to offer its staff structured group instruction in the use of computers and software. Yet this is just one component of a comprehensive program of computer training and support for library staff.

The strength of the microcomputer as a stand-alone device lies in its flexibility. Given the variety of software packages and program development environments currently available, microcomputers can assist with almost any task that involves the manipulation of numbers, text, or graphic images. The difficulty is in getting the microcomputer to do what needs to be done. Though many academic libraries have the resources to purchase microcomputers, few can double the size of their staff in order to support the machines and provide programming services. The library must, as rapidly as possible, give staff members the skills to use microcomputers reasonably independently in their work. To do so requires considered mechanisms of instruction and user support. In a large library, organizational adjustments may also be necessary.

As stated in Chapter 1, we decided to place the two full-time staff lines attached to the Microcomputer Center in an "Information Technology Section" within the library's administrative unit. The underlying logic was that the Information Technology Section (ITS) would not only administer the Microcomputer Center but play a leadership role in automation planning and encourage the adoption of microcomputer technology throughout the library. At the time the Microcomputer Center opened in spring 1984, the library possessed only two microcomputers for staff use. As of this writing, we have in place or are installing 25 workstations for our staff, in addition to the public-access machines in the Microcomputer Center and Online Classroom. Microcomputer support has thus become a major task of the Information Technology Section. It is a function a library may wish to consider in planning and budgeting for a public-access microcomputer facility. As with many of the programs described in this book, the key is to secure adequate staffing during the planning stage.

The work that the Information Technology Section performs with staff microcomputers falls into a number of broad areas. These include procurement planning, the installation and maintenance of hardware and software, training, and user support.

PROCUREMENT PLANNING

The purchase of hardware and software is obviously of great importance in starting an organization toward the use of microcomputers. Although the cost of systems continues to drop, microcomputers still represent major investments for most libraries. The selection of hardware components and software packages requires some technical expertise, which, if it is not available among staff members, the library may seek from the campus computing agency or from an external consultant. The danger in entrusting procurement decisions entirely to the resident--or external--expert is that each microcomputer system should be suited to the particular needs of the staff members who will actually use it, and the "experts" must understand these needs as well as they understand the capabilities of computers. The library also misses an opportunity to encourage staff acceptance of microcomputers if it fails to involve staff members in the thinking that precedes system purchase. Ideally, the library will manage to strike a balance between group process and technical expertise in its purchasing decisions.

At our library, a committee was established to make recommendations for the purchase of the first microcomputer systems, which were acquired before we had an Information Technology Section. The committee defined how the machines were likely to be used, studied hardware and software options, and proposed systems for purchase, with budget figures, to library administrators.

At present, the Information Technology Section is responsible for preparing automation-related budgets and for conducting procurement planning for computing equipment. Our approach in coordinating procurement is to meet first with the staff of the library units that will be affected by system purchases and to identify broadly the activities they are currently conducting with microcomputers and their plans for the future. Depending on the extent of the purchase that is proposed, we might then designate a working group of several interested staff members to work with the ITS in developing a list of equipment needed. If, for instance, the initial group consideration had identified several large database applications, an extensive use of word processing, and the occasional need to generate high-quality correspondence, the working group might conclude that the department requires, in addition to computers and dot-matrix printers, two fixed disks and a laser printer.

It would then be the business of the ITS to determine whether existing allocations will allow these purchases, to work with the working group to prioritize departmental needs if budget constraints prevent the purchase of all the desired hardware in the present budget cycle, and to identify particular products for purchase. In the area of final hardware selection and ordering, group process is minimal. The library expects the ITS to make decisions based on its technical experience, and then to support the hardware it decides to purchase.

With very minor modifications, this decision-making model applies to the procurement of software as well as hardware. In both areas, for the sake of simplicity in user support, and also to simplify the purchase of computer supplies, library administrators should seek to keep workstation hardware and software as standard and consistent as possible. In our library, one function of the ITS's involvement in the procurement process is to see that some level of consistency is maintained in meeting the needs of individual units and computer applications. This role is discussed further in the section on user support below.

In order to conduct system procurement effectively, the ITS must keep informed about emerging hardware and software products, and, in particular, about pricing. This is the practical aspect of the section's more general charge to keep abreast of emerging information technologies. Tracking the cost of computer systems in a university environment can be complex. At Cornell, for instance, hardware from several major vendors is available through Cornell Computer Services at a substantial discount, local computer stores offer systems from several other vendors to the university at competitive prices, and national mail-order outlets sometimes undercut both on certain categories of equipment. So rapidly do computer systems appear on the market and prices change, that typically the hardware configurations and costs specified in budget requests are out of date by the time the budget is approved. Thus, in a sense, every microcomputer system the library purchases must be configured at least twice, once when we ask administration to fund it, and once when we actually go out on the market to buy it.

SYSTEM INSTALLATION AND MAINTENANCE

For certain applications, it is currently possible to buy microcomputer systems that can be installed without a screwdriver--one removes the components from their boxes, connects them according to simple instructions, and plugs in the power cord. In many parts of the country, it is also possible to pay a computer store or specialist to assemble and install a computer system for you. In most cases, however, the installation of microcomputer systems requires technical expertise, not only when the hardware is assembled but when software is configured to run on the hardware that an organization has in place. It is often substantially less expensive to purchase hardware components from a number of vendors and assemble them locally than to buy ready-to-run systems from a computer store or campus outlet. A library that fails to develop some in-house expertise in microcomputer hardware and software will thus pay premium prices for its computer systems.

As the Information Technology Section has developed the skills necessary to assemble and configure microcomputer systems, we do this work in the library without the involvement of external technicians. Although we save money by taking this approach, and secure hardware systems that are specific to very particular needs, we do pay a price in staff time. Installing a hard disk subsystem in a microcomputer can take two hours or more. Configuring a database manager to run on a computer system in a way that is convenient for the staff member who uses the package can be a major task. Here, as in other areas, we have drawn on the talents of the student employees of the Microcomputer Center to supplement the library's microcomputer support services to staff. We currently have two students dedicate a total of eight hours per week to tasks related to staff workstations. This work involves preparing and filing product registrations and insurance papers for new hardware, installing microcomputer systems, configuring software packages, troubleshooting hardware and software, and performing the sorts of minor repairs that can be performed on-site.

In addition to the installation of hardware and initial configuration of software, the Information Technology Section has taken several steps to rationalize the reporting and correction of microcomputer problems. Although library staff members remain free to bring problems in person to the ITS, we maintain a written log for reporting hardware and software difficulties in the Administrative Office. This gives us a full record of the problems staff members are currently experiencing with their computers, the steps we have taken to remedy the problems, and the ways in which the difficulties were ultimately resolved. Where more than one staff member is involved in troubleshooting and user support, this approach eliminates duplication of effort and allows the computer staff to systematically prioritize repair and support activity. Hardware troubleshooting and software support can be extremely time-consuming jobs. It is thus important that computer support personnel dedicate their time to the tasks that will really make a difference in staff productivity and convenience.

As is true with the computers in the Microcomputer Center, our library pays for maintenance to staff workstations on an ongoing basis, rather than depending on maintenance contracts with a particular vendor. We also insure our hardware with the university to protect ourselves against theft. Supplies such as paper, ribbons, and diskettes represent a continuing cost of computer support. Whatever particular arrangements a library may make in these areas, some budgetary provisions need to be made for expenses that go beyond the purchase of microcomputer system hardware and software. Microcomputers can make library staff members more effective at their jobs, and they certainly have the potential to change the way in which the library accesses and processes information. Nevertheless, system purchase is just one element of the real cost of adopting this technology, and the library needs to make an ongoing budgetary commitment to the maintenance of its workstations by anticipating that maintenance and supply expenses will total at least ten percent of purchase price per year.

STAFF TRAINING

Staff training in the use of microcomputers began at the library more than a year before we opened the Microcomputer Center. In the fall of 1982, our only microcomputer was an Apple II which had an inexplicable tendency to intermittently reset itself. The library purchased its second microcomputer-- one of the early 64K IBM PCs--in February 1983. As is the case in many organizations, this machine was earmarked for placement in the Administrative Office, to be used for word-processing and spreadsheet applications. We realized, nonetheless, that there was a great deal of interest in other library departments in the potential of the microcomputer, and we felt that the library must move to educate its staff in a technology which would be in wide use within two years.

In part to arouse people's curiosity, the administrative office sent a memo to all staff members to inform them of the arrival of the new microcomputer. Attached was a brief questionnaire asking staff members about their previous computer experience, their interest in computing, and the types of applications programs they considered most appropriate in their area of work. This information was used to initiate introductory sessions in the use of applications software. Once each week, we would place the microcomputer on a book truck and roll it to a meeting room on the third floor of the library. Six or seven staff members would gather for an explanation and demonstration of a word processor, a spreadsheet, or a file manager. In all, approximately two-thirds of the library staff attended one of these sessions over a three-month period.

In order to make the microcomputer accessible to all library staff members for an individual follow-up to these introductory sessions, we set aside two one-hour time blocks during the day--one at lunch and one in mid-afternoon--when the machine was dedicated to training. Staff members signed up for the time blocks in advance on a calendar and were then welcome to make use of tutorial aids in wordprocessing and spreadsheets. As the office assistant at the time had some knowledge of microcomputers, a resource person was available to answer questions.

Within a month of purchase, staff members of the Administrative Office were using the computer almost constantly. Making the machine available for general staff education meant committing a scarce resource to a cause that was not getting today's work done. There was some pressure to drop the educational access until the library could afford more hardware, but we decided to continue the training program even if it meant paying some price in short-term productivity. This position affirmed the library's commitment to the idea that personnel in every department of the library needed access to microcomputers.

The opening of the Microcomputer Center gave the library the opportunity to expand the scope of its instructional sessions for the staff. Now we could conduct hands-on workshops for 20 or more staff members at once, allowing us to provide regular, formal group instruction in the use of microcomputers and software. We have made every effort to see that as many staff members as possible have been able to undergo classroom training. Although we require that those interested seek their supervisor's approval to attend a workshop, so that minimal staffing levels can be maintained throughout the library, we have sought to attract as many people as possible. During the first two years of the program, the library has not insisted that staff members have an immediate need for the applications package to be covered in order to attend a workshop. It is not reasonable, we feel, to require that staff members indicate how they will use a microcomputer in their work until they have gained some familiarity with what the machines can do. The structure and coverage of our workshops in applications software were covered in some detail in Chapter 12.

In addition to group instruction, the Information Technology Section does teach certain staff members the use of software packages on a one-to-one basis. This is clearly a less efficient way to teach than through classroom workshops, and a different set of criteria apply. In this case, interest on the part of the staff member alone would not justify the investment of time required to offer personal instruction. The Information Technology Section undertakes such instruction when we are convinced that a member of the library staff has a particular project that he or she can best carry forward with an improved understanding of some specific software package, and when no campus organization offers a workshop in that package.

Access to our workshops for our staff, then, has been wide open, whereas we offer personal instruction in the use of software only when we anticipate a prompt gain in staff productivity. To date, library administration has encouraged all staff members to learn how to use a microcomputer, but has not required that anyone undergo training. The projects we have undertaken with microcomputers, though they have involved the Information Technology Section in most instances, have been structured around the interests and abilities of individual staff members. We believe that this is the most reasonable approach to take in introducing a new technology that has the potential to change and even redefine many of the jobs that people perform in the library. Encouraging staff members to learn about microcomputing quickly makes it obvious who is genuinely interested in mastering the operation of a computer. Performance in workshops also provides a solid indication of which staff members have the natural analytical abilities to use software effectively. By directing its first microcomputer-based projects to these individuals, the library increases the odds of success and creates a group of skilled users who will later pass on their knowledge to others. A second advantage to a voluntary approach in training is that initially no one is forced to sit down at a microcomputer. Making participation voluntary reduces the risk of pointlessly alienating those whose ultimate support is critical to the adoption of microcomputers and library automation in general.

In the early stages of microcomputer training, our library has thus sought to foster success through self-selection. As the individuals who make the first expressions of interest in microcomputing begin to use the machines in performing their jobs, they come to enjoy a new visibility within the organization, particularly if the scope or effectiveness of their work increases because of their use of a computer. In our experience, the emergence of these first, self-motivated microcomputer users has an important effect on the way their co-workers view the technology. Example is a much more powerful inducement to change in the workplace than administrative fiat.

The library has now pursued this voluntary program of training in the use of microcomputers for two years, with solid results. We have a core of experienced users on the staff and numerous established applications running under database managers, spreadsheets, word processors, communications software, and bibliographic file managers. Microcomputers are so well established within the library, in fact, that in the near future we will have to begin revising the basis for participation in the training programs that the Information Technology Section conducts. Just as use of the RLIN terminal is part of the job in the cataloging unit, the ability to operate certain software packages on a microcomputer will become a requirement in many areas of library work. Consequently, many members of the library staff, and especially those entering positions where the use of the microcomputer is established, will have to undergo training. A challenge for us over the next year will be to move to this model without losing the healthy elements of self-motivation that have characterized our workshop program to date, and without threatening those people on staff who still do not feel comfortable with computers.

USER SUPPORT

During the next several years, libraries will have to scramble as they seek to support staff use of at least four major categories of computer systems--the bibliographic utilities, online commercial databases (both bibliographic and nonbibliographic), local online catalogs and "integrated" library systems, and microcomputers running applications software. As time goes on, of course, these four basic areas of activity will grow increasingly interwoven and difficult to separate. Still, at present it is valuable to distinguish them from one another, at least conceptually.

In several senses, local microcomputer-based applications are the most difficult of these four categories to support. Where online services and local library systems are uniform environments that change relatively slowly, microcomputers are capable of performing an exciting but sometimes bewildering array of tasks, using thousands of different applications packages. If not satisfied with what is available commercially, staff members with the necessary skills can go ahead and write their own programs. In addition to this multiplicity of software environments, the world of microcomputing is still marked by an absence of the sorts of organized training materials and programs that are available through, say, the bibliographic utilities or the commercial online services. Last but hardly least, with microcomputers, the library supports the hardware and at least installs the software. There is no BRS or DIALOG, no OCLC or RLIN, to do it for you. With microcomputers, the library must find its own way.

When training in the use of microcomputers is successful, it leads staff members to employ software in the performance of their jobs. This success does not conclude the staff support that a unit like the Information Technology Section must offer in microcomputing. In an important sense, this is just the beginning. The complexity of microcomputer software is such that staff operators usually encounter frustrating obstacles as they try to learn the operation of a package, and they continue to have questions, of increasing sophistication, as their experience grows. The result is a need to provide ongoing user support. The Information Technology Section in our library attempts to resolve computing problems and to encourage staff projects on microcomputers wherever possible, though limits are imposed by our current level of staffing and the demands of operating the Microcomputer Center.

Most microcomputer users feel that computing problems cannot wait. When one is stuck in a software program, it may prove impossible to "work around the problem" precisely because one does not understand exactly what has happened. Staff members may believe that valuable data is in danger of corruption or simply feel frustrated by the complexities of the technology they are using. This situation poses a dilemma. To assist and encourage staff who are working with microcomputers, computing support personnel should respond to every plea for help immediately. If they do so consistently, though, they may find themselves without the time to do their own jobs, and potentially without the time to move the organization forward in a broad sense. Furthermore, computer users may become dependent on staff specialists with more expertise for the resolution of all problems, which does not lead to the independence the library is seeking to foster. These concerns admit the possibility of several administrative approaches, and a library may wish to adapt a number of mechanisms for the provision of staff support.

First, a library of any size should seek to place on its staff someone with computer skills and designate that person as the primary support person for microcomputers and software. This activity may not occupy the entirety of this staff member's time, but administration should set aside hours for support work and write the responsibility clearly into the person's job description. Microcomputer technology is increasingly central to information access and retrieval, and a library can no longer afford to treat it in an ad hoc manner.

In addition to professional support, the library should encourage the development of less formal mechanisms of software consulting within the departments of the library. Corporations have taken this approach by designating "super users" or "power users" throughout the organization. These individuals serve as a first line of consulting support and as a users group that maintains communication between the microcomputer support personnel in the data-processing department or information center and the staff as a whole. Libraries can profitably borrow this model. Through training programs and the normal course of events, certain staff members in each department will show an aptitude for microcomputing and become leaders in utilizing the technology. Library administrators should encourage these people to act as coaches and consultants in a way that serves to disseminate their knowledge without unduly interfering with their line duties. Library administrators should recognize that within a very few years, it will not be a "bonus" but a requirement that employees possess a full range of computer skills. The development of these skills justifies some sacrifice in daily productivity as measured by traditional standards.

To foster consistency and reduce the complexity of the support function, the library should exercise some control over the use of software on staff computers. Variety may be the spice of life, but it is agony for software support personnel. Although directors should encourage departments to think creatively about the solution of information-processing problems with a computer, they should seek to limit the number of software packages used to perform the same function within the library. In addition to preventing an unnecessary proliferation of software "solutions," careful record-keeping and purchasing procedures insure that the organization is using software legitimately and that it is registered with vendors for upgrades and technical support.

In making decisions about software acquisition, the library should give some consideration to the overall campus environment, some consideration to the avowed "special" needs of departmental applications, and substantial consideration to maintaining consistency throughout the organization. In all but the largest libraries, one person should probably review all software purchase requests. Preferably, this person will also be directly involved in microcomputer support, so that he or she understands the computing environment, and suffers the consequences of mistakes.

The library typically will want to update its software to reflect the vendor's latest version and will purchase new packages as they become clear "winners." The major purpose of introducing microcomputers into the processing operations of the library is not to test new software products, however; it is to control effectively the flow of information. This implies a conservative approach to purchases for staff use, as opposed to purchases intended for public access collections. The software running on staff machines should be standard, proven, and widely supported.

Wherever possible, the library should provide broad staff access to microcomputer hardware and software for self-instruction. Our own efforts in this area were described earlier in the chapter. Implicit here is an idea stated above: initially, library administrators should not insist that staff members be able to explain where they will use a microcomputer in their work. It is often impossible to make this judgment until one has gained familiarity with the behavior of actual software packages.

In addition to offering individual consulting support, the Information Technology Section has provided programming assistance to several microcomputer projects. Examples include a program developed under dBase III to provide fund accounting, not currently available through RLIN, to the library's Collection Development Department, a system that tracks staff vacation and sick leave hours for the Administrative Office, and a database system that maintains records of library-owned equipment. Students from the staff of the Microcomputer Center have written programs in support of these and several other projects. Recently, we have secured grant monies separate from the budget of the Microcomputer Center to allow the library to hire more student programmers. Although the efforts of student programmers require careful planning and review on the part of full-time personnel, an academic library may wish to consider this method of augmenting its own staff resources.

The Information Technology Section tries to keep the entire staff informed of developments and opportunities in computing. These range from the availability of new software packages to training programs conducted on the Cornell campus. When we have information that is of general interest, such as a schedule of workshops for staff instruction, a memo goes out to all library staff members. In a larger library, a regular newsletter on microcomputing might be valuable.

Effective support for microcomputing within a library is part planning, part salesmanship, part technical consulting, part cheerleading, and part seduction. One last technique that we have found effective is to give visibility to the achievements of those who have worked hard to automate their jobs by involving them in presentations to other staff members and to outside groups. This recognition at once rewards the efforts of the presenter and acts to motivate the audience. Moving large portions of one's work to a microcomputer is not easy. The organization that requires this step should try to boost morale together with productivity.

SUMMARY

1. Although the potential of the microcomputer as a staff tool in the academic library environment is now beyond doubt, the technology remains complex and requires considered mechanisms of instruction and support. The introduction and support of microcomputing may require organizational adjustments in a large library.

2. The placement of computer support staff in the library's organizational chart will strongly influence the role they can play. Placement of the staff of a microcomputer center in the administrative unit allows these individuals to address the microcomputing and automation needs of the entire organization, rather than limiting them to public service functions. The work that computer support staff members perform in the area of microcomputing may be divided into procurement planning, the installation and maintenance of hardware and software, training, and user support.

3. The evaluation and selection of microcomputer system components requires technical skills. In addition, the person who makes the decisions on system purchase must be highly familiar with the needs of the staff members who will be using individual workstations. Group process is appropriate in the initial definition of the uses to which particular workstations will be put, in part because this insures that the "expert" understands the needs of the end-user, and in part because involvement in the process that leads to system purchase encourages staff members to accept the new technology willingly .

4. Unlike the definition of system requirements, the selection of particular computer components for purchase should be entrusted to staff specialists. This model applies to software as well as to hardware. Therefore the computer support staff needs to keep abreast of products and pricing in the microcomputer marketplace. Through the role played in system procurement by the staff specialists, a library can minimize needless proliferation of types of hardware and software.

5. In-house expertise in assembling and configuring microcomputer systems will save a library money and increase its flexibility in procuring hardware. The installation and configuration of software packages is also far from straightforward in many cases. Student employees can often save professional time in these areas. Libraries with large numbers of staff workstations may also want to institute a formal procedure for the reporting and resolution of problems with microcomputer systems.

6. Without requiring attendance, library administrators do well to encourage their staff to take workshops in the use of microcomputers and software. The library should not insist that staff members be able to demonstrate an immediate need for a particular software package in order to attend a training session. Staff members must gain exposure to micro-computing before they can make reasonable judgments as to how useful the technology might prove in their jobs, or whether they want to put it to use.

7. Although attendance at workshops should be as free as is practical, one-to-one instruction may be justified only when computer support personnel are convinced that a staff member has a project that he or she can best carry forward with a particular piece of software. A library should

encourage those of the staff who demonstrate an aptitude for computing in a training program to undertake work-related projects. By directing pilot projects to highly motivated staff members, a library increases the odds of success and creates a core group of skilled users.

8. As a library succeeds in adopting microcomputer technology, the rationale for participation in the training program may have to change. In certain positions, the use of a microcomputer is already a requirement, and this trend will grow stronger over the next few years.

9. Support activity in microcomputing must strike a balance between the need to move promptly to help the staff member who is encountering trouble and the need to develop a staff of competent and self-sufficient computer users. In most cases, a library should officially designate someone as the primary source of user support in microcomputing and write the responsibility into this individual's job description. Less formal systems of support--such as networks of "power users" and the employment of student "experts"--are also mechanisms worth consideration.

10. Certain staff members in each department will show an aptitude for microcomputing. The library should encourage these people to provide leadership and consulting support to other staff members. The importance of effectively adopting microcomputer technology may justify a short-term drop in staff productivity as measured by traditional standards.

11. In user support, as in hardware procurement and maintenance, some reasonable degree of consistency throughout the organization is essential. In the staff use of applications software, in contrast to the development of a public-access collection, buying the latest package is not the point. The goal is to increase the ability of the library to access and manipulate information.

Conclusion

Howard Curtis and Jan Olsen

The Microcomputer Center has significantly broadened the spectrum of activities that patrons conduct within Mann Library. In addition to the library's print resources and traditional reference tools, students and faculty members can make use of microcomputer software on library machines. Patrons now perform data analysis and write research papers in close proximity to the information resources that they depend on.

Increasingly, microcomputers also provide patrons of an academic library with direct access to computerized sources of research information, as well as with the capability to manipulate subsets of that information locally. It is because of these developments in the academic applications of computing that our library offers end-user instruction in searching online databases, and why we have moved that program, over the course of the past two years, from dumb terminals to microcomputers. In the next year, the library will make available microcomputers that support scholarly indexes on compact disk, again expanding the range of knowledge that can be accessed through a microcomputer. When the Cornell University libraries implement an online catalog, it too will be available, through a local area network, to patrons working at the microcomputers in the Micro Center.

These represent major advances in library facilities, in the scope of information instruction offered in the library, and in the ways in which the library offers access to the information in its collection. Nevertheless, the true potential of the microcomputer as a scholar's workstation will not be realized so long as the locus of library-supported activity is limited to the library building.

For instance, while one clear advantage of an online catalog is that it provides users with multiple points of access to the library's bibliographic database and with other powerful techniques of refining searches of that database, a second major strength is that an online catalog, supported by a campus network, is ubiquitously available--in the library, in faculty offices and laboratories, and in student dormitories. Though this point may be widely accepted as it pertains to an online catalog, the same logic applies to the sorts of facilities and resources that we have begun to put in place with the Microcomputer Center. Researchers who must come to the library to search the MEDLINE database on compact disk are not fully served by computer technology. Students with microcomputers in their dormitory rooms who must walk to the Microcomputer Center and stand in line to use reserve software packages to complete assignments will legitimately complain that there should be a better way.

When microcomputers first appeared at Cornell--and on other campuses--their attraction was precisely their local processing capability. Micros made the user independent of the complexities of the large university computing system. It was no longer necessary to struggle with a line editor to write one's master's thesis. Graduate students confronted with the need to perform statistical analyses of laboratory data did not have to find funding sources for "research computing." Faculty members who wished to integrate computing into introductory courses could avoid the administrative difficulties of establishing computer "accounts" for large numbers of students.

Despite these attractions of local processing it has nevertheless become obvious in the last few years that a microcomputer which is strictly local in its capabilities does not fully exploit the new technology. Researchers want to extract information from large, remote databases for local manipulation. Students wish not only to write their papers with a computer but also to communicate with each other and with their instructors and to search the library catalogs. Even departmental offices, which in the first instance may have begun developing budgets with spreadsheet programs running on microcomputers, now want access to university accounting files through the same machines, as they seek to increase the control they exercise over their funds.

To make these sorts of computing possible, a university must move from a model in which mainframe-based computing and microcomputing are separate to "distributed" computing, where the microcomputer can function as a local processor and gain access to shared computing resources. The microcomputer is at once a stand-alone device and an intelligent terminal on the campus computing network. From the perspective of the research library, it is only with the transition to distributed computing in this sense that the microcomputer can begin to function as a scholar's workstation for information access and retrieval.

The movement to a true distributed computing environment requires two steps: the installation of the cabling and hardware that allow microcomputers located throughout university buildings to enter the campus network, and the development of access, storage, and training mechanisms that encourage students, faculty, and staff to take advantage of the information resources now available to them. Cornell, like many universities, has made substantial progress in both areas in the last year. These developments have implications for the future of microcomputing in the libraries and are thus worth outlining here.

In addition to modem-supported communications through the telephone system, Cornell Computer Services has operated a broadband data communications network for approximately ten years. This network linked public terminal clusters and certain administrative offices to the university mainframe computers but was never extended to many campus buildings. In 1985, the university purchased and installed a new campus telephone system, which is controlled by the institution, rather than by New York Telephone. Together with voice communications, this system gives the university the option of providing substantial data transmission capabilities wherever telephones are located in campus buildings. When the cable for this new telephone system was installed, the university also laid coaxial cable and duct for fiber-optic lines to each building on the Cornell campus, to simplify future network installations.

This cabling is now providing the basis for the development of two high-speed data communications networks, one to connect research laboratories with special needs to the university's new supercomputer facility and one to support general academic computing. A gateway will link the two networks. In addition to these on-campus networks, the campus computing system provides access to national telecommunications links such as BITNET and TELENET. The State of New York is pushing forward with plans for a high-speed network called NYSERNET that will link the libraries and laboratories of Cornell and other research institutions with major industrial research centers.

Planning efforts designed to further the use of computer technology for the control of scholarly information have begun in the past year at both the university and college level. The Provost has convened a task force consisting of faculty, administrators, and librarians to assess how the university can best encourage and support scholarship in an increasingly automated environment. The group conceptualized computer-based sources of scholarly information at a research institution as constituting a set of concentric rings. In the central circle are found computers, mass-storage devices, telecommunications connections, and technical experts. This computing resource directly supports databases of importance to scholars and facilitates access to information located outside the institution. Around this center lies a ring of data providers, who make use of the central facilities to create significant information resources, such as databases or expert systems, and information analysts and interpreters, including librarians, who offer consultation and support to faculty and research groups. Around this ring in turn are the faculty and students who are the consumers of the information resources of the university. Under this model, experts in hardware, networking, and other technical aspects of computing will cooperate closely with personnel trained in the creation of databases and in teaching users to handle computerized information resources efficiently. Because of the evolving relationship between computer and information professionals, the possibility of bringing the Cornell libraries and Cornell Computer Services closer together interested the task force.

Within the College of Agriculture and Life Sciences, in an example of related activity at the college level, the Dean of the College convened an Agricultural Information Systems Committee which met throughout 1985. This committee considered the automated information needs of the college in the areas of research, instruction, and extension. Among the recommendations of the committee was the creation of an online information system for the college, probably supported by a minicomputer, that would provide access to locally developed databases and function as a gateway to external sources of computerized information. The committee also recommended that college funds be invested in creating, testing, and disseminating research databases, that a systematic program of training in the nature and use of information systems be put in place, and that the faculty and staff be assisted in securing microcomputers with the communication capabilities necessary to take advantage of online information systems.

As the campus network comes into broad use and as significant sources of scholarly information become available through the university computing system, researchers and students will, with increasing frequency, use microcomputers to locate and retrieve the information that they need in their work. The campus-wide availability of a library's online catalog is one obvious example of this trend, but the university will also mount on its computers large databases developed in the course of research projects or purchased from national information sources. The university computing network will include gateways that allow researchers to gain access to commercial information utilities. Collections of microcomputer software, where licensing arrangements allow, will be placed online for downloading to student microcomputers.

The development of this network-based information environment, which should be substantially in place within two to three years, will lead librarians to assume new duties in administering and supporting the information resources of the university. The nature of public-access microcomputing in the academic library will also change in response to these trends. Certain functions that the Microcomputer Center provides today will move elsewhere as networked microcomputing becomes the rule at Cornell. As the price of entry-level machines drops, for example, and more students purchase their own systems, word processing will leave public facilities in favor of student dormitories and apartments. Those who require course-reserve software to complete an assignment will locate the software they need on a network file-server, download the program to their own computer, and then run it locally. In this environment, the staff of the Microcomputer Center will loan fewer diskettes to patrons over the counter and instead will work with the faculty to insure that software is made available through the campus network as it is needed.

These predictions might seem to suggest that networked microcomputing spells the death of public-access computing facilities--in libraries as well as elsewhere on campus. We are not concerned by this prospect. While the emergence of a fully functional campus network may reduce the number of students who crowded the Microcomputer Center in the last year, it will actually allow us to better perform the role we feel we should be playing. First, group instruction will continue to be an efficient way to train students and researchers in the use of information technology. The increase in microcomputing activity on campus and the continued movement of research information to machine-readable form will simply make the need for the sorts of instruction the library offers more acute. While commonly used software may be accessed through the network, the Microcomputer Center's software collection will continue to fulfill an important and perhaps expanded function for those patrons who are looking for a piece of software that meets their specific needs.

The library's work in the systematic review of software will also grow in importance as a larger proportion of the university community comes to depend on the functionality of microcomputer software. Finally, the work of library professionals as consultants in the use of computerized information systems--a role that is directly supported by the presence of the Microcomputer Center in the building--will become an ever larger part of the job of Public Services staff in the next few years. In three vital areas--instruction, collection, and consultation with patrons--we anticipate that the Microcomputer Center will continue to play a vital, if changing, role in the pattern of library services. It will take years of intensive support of this kind before the microcomputer comes to be used to anything approaching its potential in research or instruction. The academic library has an opportunity to make a strong contribution to the adoption of microcomputer technology if the library acts now.

Appendix

What follows is a selection of documents related to the development of the software library in the Mann Library Microcomputer Center. The first is a reserve policy statement for microcomputer software that we have distributed to departmental chairpersons in our colleges.

RESERVE POLICY FOR SOFTWARE

Purpose

One purpose of Mann Library in establishing the Mann Library Microcomputer Center was to support efforts to expand the scope of academic computing in the College of Agriculture and Life Sciences and the College of Human Ecology. A variety of courses that have not previously used computing are introducing a component based on the microcomputer into the semester's work. In order to make these exercises as effective and convenient as possible for students, Mann will hold microcomputer software in the Microcomputer Center on a reserve loan basis. Policies for these materials parallel those of the Reserve Department wherever possible, but the problems posed by microcomputers and microcomputer software make some new rules inevitable.

Mann Library will house and circulate reserve software for courses in the College of Agriculture and Life Sciences, the College of Human Ecology, the Division of Nutritional Sciences, the Division of Biological Sciences, and for programs of CALS, CHE, DNS, DBS, Cooperative Extension, and the Cornell University Libraries. Other organizations are eligible only by special arrangement.

Procedure

To put a software package on reserve for the first time faculty must consult with the Micro Center Manager or the Computerized Data Services Librarian. Subsequent reserve use of the same material can be initiated by telephone or mail.

Funding and shelving

Mann Library's budget for microcomputer software acquisition is limited. Because of the high cost of many software packages, academic departments will in many cases be expected to fund, or participate in the funding of, software required to support their courses or instructional programs. Subject to the availability of funds:

For commercial software programs:

1. Mann Library will provide one copy of a program, or sets of programs, for every 20 students registered for the course, to a maximum of ten packages.
2. The maximum dollar amount that can be allotted to any one course is $300.00, including the costs of documentation.
3. The maximum number of diskettes that can be included in a course reserve package is six.

For public domain software:

1. Mann Library will make packages available to students on a reserve basis, but will not seek to actively support the use of the software.
2. The limitations on numbers are identical to those applied to commercial programs.
3. Public domain software is understood to include software developed by Cornell faculty or staff. Mann Library acknowledges and respects the developer's right to market such software externally, but will not pay for such programs when they are to be placed on reserve.

Software support

1. Mann Library requires that the faculty member requesting a reserve placement provide an appropriate number of diskettes, ready to run.

Note that this means the diskettes should be properly configured to operate in the Mann Microcomputer Center's hardware environment (we have, for example, serial printers which will not respond to "default" software configurations). We strongly suggest that programs be tested on the Microcomputer Center's hardware before copies are produced. Material should be turned over to the staff of the Microcomputer Center at least two weeks before students will need to use it, so that the library may make provisions for storage and access. The library expects faculty to obtain approval from software vendors for the use in a public-access environment of all packages placed on reserve.

    2. Reasonable documentation should be provided to students who will use reserve programs in the Microcomputer Center. We recommend that copies be distributed in lecture. Additionally, copies must also be turned over to the library as part of the reserve packet. Documentation for each loan kit should include a set of instructions sufficient to guide the user to the point where the application program is running.

    3. The student operators of the Microcomputer Center will provide assistance to patrons when they require help in starting an application. However, our staff cannot be expected to provide consulting support in the operation of the program itself when the reserve package is a locally developed or subject-specific application. If students in a course will require such support, the academic department must anticipate providing a teaching assistant in the Microcomputer Center as necessary. Please consult with Mann Library before establishing a schedule for the presence of a teaching assistant in the center. Our use patterns dictate that such software consultation will normally have to take place between 7:00 pm and 11:45 pm.

Software ownership

    If the reserve package was bought by Mann Library it will be cataloged and added to the collection.

    If the package was bought by departmental funds faculty have two alternatives:

    1.   The material can be donated to the library, and it will be added to the collection, if it is within our collection scope.

    2.   Ownership can be retained by the department and the software brought to the Microcomputer Center each semester it is to be placed on reserve. The Microcomputer Center will permanently shelve only library owned packages.

LETTER TO VENDORS

The following is a copy of the letter mailed to vendors of software packages that the library wishes to purchase for the Microcomputer Center's software collection. The letter accompanies the Cornell University purchase order forwarded to the vendor by Cornell Purchasing.

Dear Sirs:

Mann Library, the library of the Colleges of Agriculture and Human Ecology at Cornell University, would like to purchase ____ copies of the program _____ for use in our Microcomputer Center.

The Mann Library Microcomputer Center contains 35 microcomputers (29 IBM PCs, two DEC Rainbows, and four Apple Macintoshes) for the use of the faculty, students, and staff of Cornell University. In addition to providing support for course work and a comprehensive instructional program, the center loans software for use on its machines. No commercial software diskettes may leave the premises of the center.

Our center is staffed full time to ensure that our operational policies are enforced. Signs that specify the illegality of copying licensed software are displayed at the loan counter and at every workstation. Students are made to understand that they risk their borrowing privileges in the Microcomputer Center should they conduct unauthorized copying of diskettes.

Since the Microcomputer Center contains 35 machines we are not able to tie the use of individual software packages to individual machines, but we do not run more copies of a program simultaneously than we have purchased.

The Mann Library Microcomputer Center is a recognized pioneer among microcomputer facilities in academic libraries, and we are aware of the precedents we set. The attached document states our Microcomputer Center's policies regarding the use of commercial software. We trust that these terms will be acceptable to you. Our rules are intended to protect the legitimate interests of software producers, while allowing us the flexibility we need to operate the Microcomputer Center.

Should these terms not be acceptable to you, or should you desire clarification, please contact Mann Library before filling the attached order.

Sincerely yours,

PURCHASE AGREEMENT FOR SOFTWARE

The following enumerates Mann Library's policies regarding the use of commercial software packages in the Micro Center. This statement accompanies the letter reproduced above.

1. Software will be used on Microcomputer Center machines only.
2. We will not run more copies of a program simultaneously than we have purchased.
3. Diskettes will remain in the Microcomputer Center at all times. Documentation may be checked out on overnight loan.
4. Injunctions against the copying of software are posted at the loan counter and at every workstation. Each program diskette boots up with a similar injunction. Patrons are warned that they risk their borrowing privileges in the center should they conduct unauthorized copying of programs.
5. Software is only loaned to members of the Cornell University community.

INJUNCTIONS AGAINST COPYING COMMERCIAL SOFTWARE

This injunction is posted at every workstation in the Microcomputer Center.

Commercial software is to be used only in the Microcomputer Center and is not to be copied under any circumstances. Violation of these rules may result in the suspension of your borrowing privileges within the Microcomputer Center.

This injunction is included in the "autoexec" batch file on all program diskettes in the Microcomputer Center's software collection. This text appears on screen when a patron runs an applications program borrowed from our collection.

Please Note:

**All diskettes and documentation are the property of Mann Library.

**No Micro Center diskettes may be removed from the Micro Center.

**No commercial software programs in our collection may be copied for use outside the Micro Center.

**We will report violations of these rules to the Cornell judicial administrator. Copying commercial software programs may also result in the suspension of your borrowing privileges within the Micro Center.

Index

The authors of this book are nine full-time members of the staff of Mann Library, Cornell University. As the people most closely involved in establishing the programs and policies of the Microcomputer Center, they represent all library units: Collection Development, Public Services, Technical Services, Administration, and the Information Technology Section. The creation of the Microcomputer Center, together with the development of the library's software collection and instructional programs, has been throughout a cooperative effort on the part of these individuals and departments.

The nine chapter authors currently hold the following positions at Mann Library:

Katherine Chiang -- Computerized Data Services Librarian
Bill Coons -- Information Literacy Specialist
Howard Curtis -- Head, Information Technology Section
Samuel Demas -- Head, Collection Development
Joan Lippincott -- Head, Public Services
James Madden -- Microcomputer Center Manager
Mary Ochs -- Document Delivery Librarian
Jan Olsen -- Director, Mann Library
Linda Stewart -- Online Coordinator